362.708
C536   Auerbach
v.4   Child care

Glendale College
Library

SPECIAL NEEDS AND SERVICES

CHILD CARE:
A COMPREHENSIVE GUIDE

A SERIES

Edited by
Stevanne Auerbach, Ph. D.

with
James A. Rivaldo

SPECIAL NEEDS AND SERVICES

Philosophy, Programs, and Practices for the Creation of Quality
Service for Children

VOLUME FOUR
in the Series
CHILD CARE:
A COMPREHENSIVE GUIDE

Edited by
Stevanne Auerbach, Ph.D.
with
James A. Rivaldo

Foreword by
Jeannette Watson
Director,
Early Childhood Development Division
Texas Department of Community Affairs

362.908
C536
V. 4

Copyright © 1979 by Stevanne Auerbach

All rights reserved. No part of this work may be reproduced or utilized in any form or by any means, electronic or mechanical, including photocopying, microfilm and recording, or by any information storage and retrieval system without permission in writing from the publisher.

HUMAN SCIENCES PRESS
72 Fifth Avenue
New York, New York 10011

Printed in the United States of America
9 987654321

Library of Congress Cataloging in Publication Data (Revised)

Auerbach, Stevanne.
   Child care—a comprehensive guide.

   (v. 2 Early childhood series)
   Vol. 2 lacks subtitle.
   Includes bibliographies.
   CONTENTS: v. 2. Rationale for child care services: programs vs. politics.—v. 2. Model programs and their components.—v. 3.   —v. 4. Special needs and services.
   1. Child welfare—United States—Collected works. I. Rivaldo, James A., joint author. II. Title. III. Series: Early childhood series (New York)
HV741.A94   362.7'08   LC 74-28029
ISBN: 0–87705–349–9

To the parents now using child care and to those who will need the services in the future.

PREFACE TO VOLUME IV

This volume of *Child Care: A Comprehensive Guide* discusses methods for responding to young children who have special needs, or who are disabled or abused. The emphasis is on working effectively with parents, minorities, and teenagers, and creating programs for the development of a responsive delivery of services to all families in need.

Stevanne Auerbach

CONTENTS

FOREWORD

A children's book from the Mister Rogers Neighborhood television program tells of a king who decreed that everyone should look alike.

"I order all of you," he told his subjects, "to wear masks of my face and put on robes like mine."

What he hoped would make life simpler actually made it more confusing: he couldn't find anyone he wanted, and no one believed he was the real king. He finally realized that we're different for a reason: we're each individual, and therefore, special; his job was to help people be the best they can be.

The desire to fulfill the potential of every child to grow up to be the best person he or she can be was one of the sentiments underlying the creation of 17 state offices of child development between 1969 and 1974. They focused attention on the early years of life as a time dramatically affecting children who might otherwise grow up to be poor, retarded, or doomed to failure. Those offices had a common purpose: to help provide for the planning and coordination of adequate services to young children and their families.

On the surface, "planning and coordination" seem too bland, too far removed from reality to do anything toward helping children grow up to be the best persons they can be. To the social worker who sees helpless victims of child abuse, planning is another delay in the morass of government red tape. To the white-collar public administrator, planning is an elite scientific skill used for the good of society. Practically speaking, planning is the way we answer the question, *Who gets what?* And in a world where resources are limited and citizen groups are pressuring for their own interests, planning is essential.

We in Texas have learned that planning is most effective if linked with action. When we were doing a statewide assessment of children's needs in 1972, we were also building an information system that stands today as the only central source of statistics on children and families in Texas. While we were developing a state plan for enhancing delivery of children's services, we were conducting 13 local demonstration projects. As we surveyed child care needs in 1973, we were also developing pilot training programs for child care personnel working toward the new national Child Development Associate credential. Four years later, we can point to formal CDA training programs in 45 community colleges throughout the state, published *CDA Instructional Materials,* and more than 250 credentialed CDAs, 30 percent of whom have reported a salary increase since receiving the credential. In effect, our office has enabled more Texas communities to help children grow up to be the best persons they can be.

Hand in hand with the action orientation of our planning was the idea that we couldn't do it alone. Nor should we have to, because there were five or six state agencies already in the business of serving children. This is where coordination came in. From the time our office was established in Texas, we worked closely with a Governor-appointed committee of state agency representatives. We were also careful to incorporate citizen participation in our efforts. Our experience has shown that citizen input paints a truer picture of children's needs and at the same time builds support for policies and programs that evolve.

With citizen input, the interagency committee formulated Texas' first public policy on young children. That policy is that families hold the primary responsibility for meeting children's needs and that communities, with assistance from state and federal governments, should ensure that families have what they need to rear their children properly—to help their children become the best they can be. Why the family as primary? Because the family is the first and continuing influence on a child. Why the community? Because the community, with its schools, hospitals and churches, is where children receive services.

A public policy of the kind we have in Texas speaks to the pluralism inherent in the American tradition. Communities are different, just as people are different. Communities differ in their needs and in attitudes about how needs should be met. Texas offers a good example. In the dusty towns along the Rio Grande border, the most urgent need of children might be better health care. In the verdant but isolated hamlets of the East Texas Piney Woods, the major need may be for toys, books, and other learning materials. Child care needs in some crowded neighborhoods of Houston may best be filled by a child care center in a low-cost housing project. But in the flatlands of West Texas, where one-windmill towns are separated by miles of highways, the best solution may be a system of rural family day homes.

How can communities best interact with state and federal governments to improve services for children? We're not sure. That is the subject of a federal, state, and local interagency collaboration project now underway in Texas and South Dakota. Undoubtedly, a key issue will be how to build consensus about where we are going and what we will do for young children.

This book, which describes special needs of children and families, is valuable for decision makers and citizens alike. It provides an insight into the special needs of ethnic children and those who are handicapped or abused. It also explores the universal need of all children for informed, caring parents and parent substitutes. This book, and the three which preceded it, can help clarify the challenge of matching individual needs of children with meaningful and effective services in their communities. Paraphrasing from the king of the Neighborhood of Make-Believe, we should be concerned not with making communities the same, but with helping them be the best place for children that they can be.

Jeannette Watson

Director,
Early Childhood Development Division
Texas Department of Community Affairs
Austin, Texas

INTRODUCTION

Parent participation and community involvement form the basis on which quality child care programs function. To serve truly as an extension of the child's home life, and neither as a substitute nor a source of conflict, the child care program must receive a constant flow of information about the family life of each of its children, to ensure that it serves their needs as well as possible. Since most child care clients alone cannot afford the costs of child care, child care providers must look to community support and resources to maintain their programs. In most cases, child care providers must take the initiative in communicating with the families they serve, in seeking out the health and education professionals who can make essential contributions to their programs, and in soliciting the business and industries that can provide additional financial and material support.

In most cases, the availability of openings in child care programs determines whether mothers can seek and maintain employment or continue their education. Each mother has her own particular needs, desires, and problems, so to serve them, child care programs must be flexible and responsive. And to be responsive, child care programs must involve all parents in their activities. However, many of the problems of the family often directly prevent parents from participating.

The nation's public school systems, especially in an era of declining school-age enrollments, offer tremendous potential for meeting the need for preschool child care. Ida Bucher and Docia Zavitkovsky describe, in detail, the Santa Monica Children's Centers, which since 1943 have been administered by the California State Department of Education and the local school district. Their account of the Santa Monica experience is illustrated by a narrative of a typical day in one of the centers, as well as by copies of the official schedules of the centers.

Francione Lewis proposes a curriculum whereby high school students could earn credit for their work with children in child care settings. Seeing high school students as a vast untapped resource for child care, Ms. Lewis also suggests that work in child care programs might prepare young people for more responsible and successful parenthood.

Lucille Gold explores the process by which child care personnel prepare themselves for their career. The first step is introspective, learning who you are, and the successive steps involve learning what you do in the child care situation, learning what you need to know, and, finally, learning how to acquire the information you need. The chapter includes an extensive chart of typical child behavior and child development between birth and age eight.

Carol Hardgrove examines the role of play in the physical, mental, and social development of children. Often adult perceptions of play do not acknowledge the importance of free choice in enabling children to explore and expand their capabilities. The delicate balance between structured supervision by adults and childrens' initiatives requires constant attention by child care providers, and Ms.

Hardgrove sets forth useful guidelines for childrens' playthings and activities.

Dolly Lynch Wolverton describes the Education for Parenthood Program initiated by the HEW Office of Child Development and Office of Education in 1972, by which public schools and voluntary organizations train teenagers in child development and provide opportunities for them to work with young children in a variety of preschools and child care settings. The work-study curriculum in child development, called "exploring childhood," has been tested in hundreds of communities nationwide, and has gained the enthusiastic support of teachers, parents, teenagers, and young children everywhere.

Elsa Ten Broeck reports on the Extended Family Center, established to deal with the special problems of abused and battered children. The Center provided a full range of support services to families in which emotional instability resulted in the tragic neglect and even injury of young, helpless children at the hands of their parents. One remedy for such child abuse is the preventive measure of creating more comprehensive services such as this model demonstration project.

Lottie Rosen describes the program at Berkeley's Early Growth Center, a pioneer project that demonstrates that handicapped children can participate in regular programs. She makes specific suggestions about staffing, facilities, and daily schedules.

James A. Johnson, Jr. analyzes the reasons why the black community is increasingly involved with child care programs and suggests guidelines for determining whether these programs nurture or conflict with the socioculture values of low-income black families. Central to these guidelines is a system by which child care providers and parents can evaluate the appropriateness and effectiveness of a program.

Oscar Uribe, Mila Pascual, Roderick Auyang, and

James A. Johnson emphasize the necessity for incorporating aspects of the third world child's family milieu into his or her day care program. Each of these chapters points out special considerations that child care providers must bear in mind in order to gain the support of these children's parents.

Daniel Safran suggests ways in which parents can be encouraged to participate actively in child care programs, and he proposes some specific activities that would best use their time and effort.

Patricia Siegel describes the services developed by the Child Care Switchboard of San Francisco to assist parents in locating dependable child care.

Joan M. Bergstrom and Gwen Morgan discuss the need to develop community child care programs by coordinating the efforts of the broad range of social service and education agencies and directing them toward preventive services. The authors contend that programs geared to the vital needs of young children and their families should be the objective of comprehensive planning.

Stevanne Auerbach, in conclusion, focuses on the aspirations for the future of child care services. She suggests some of the steps that must be taken to meet the anticipated need for these services. Auerbach describes the long-range benefits of expanded child-care services, one means of financing these programs, and the delicate and challenging task of coordinating the various forces on behalf of child care.

Stevanne Auerbach

CONTRIBUTORS TO VOLUME IV

STEVANNE AUERBACH, Ph.D., is a consultant, writer and planner of child care and educational services located in San Francisco and the founder of the Institute for Childhood Resources. She conceived and developed this series in response to the gap in information about child care services. Dr. Auerbach has been in California since leaving Washington, D.C., working on behalf of families who need the services described throughout these volumes.

RODERICK AUYANG, a native of mainland China, received his degree in economics from the University of San Francisco. He served as a coordinator of a bilingual, bicultural teacher training program in Chinatown, San Francisco, and has worked for Head Start, child care, and the San Francisco Unified School District.

JOAN M. BERGSTROM, Ed.D., is Chairperson for the Early Childhood Education Department at Wheelock College in Boston, Massachusetts. Since 1972 as Associate Professor, she has been Coordinator of Wheelock's Toddler Behavior and Development Program at both the undergraduate and graduate levels. Joan Bergstrom has done extensive writing on child care delivery systems in Sweden and on the general area of early learning.

IDA M. BUCHER, currently the Director of the First Presbyterian Church School in Santa Monica, California, and instructor in Child Development at Santa Monica College, has served as a consultant and evaluator of children's centers and as the head teacher in a school-age center.

LUCILLE GOLD has spent many years teaching parents, young children, and teachers of young children and parents. She has served as a teacher and director of preschools and nursery schools in California, most recently taught early childhood education at San Jose State University, and currently produces and teaches television courses through Canada College in Redwood City.

CAROL HARDGROVE teaches about play in the Department of Family Health Care Nursing, University of California, San Francisco. Before joining the UCSF faculty, Ms. Hardgrove taught in and directed nursery school programs in day care centers, parent cooperatives, and therapeutic nursery schools. She serves as a liaison with parents' groups for the Association for the Care of Children in Hospitals, having founded the Northern California chapter of that organization.

JAMES A. JOHNSON, JR., Ph.D., is the former Director of Home-School Relations of the Far West Laboratory and former Associate Superintendent for Planning, Research and Evaluation of the Washington, D.C., public schools. He is currently the Director of Instruction Program for Educational Leaders, Nova University, Ft. Lauderdale, Florida.

FRANCIONE LEWIS, Program Director of Follow Through and previously with Education Beginning at Age Three, for the Far West Laboratory for Educational Research and Development, has a varied background in teaching, child care, and preschool education. As an advisor to the Oakland Head Start Program and as a Consultant to the Parent Child Center of West Oakland, Ms. Lewis has conducted training sessions for teaching staffs of day care centers and nursery schools, stressing developmental education, communicating, and working with parents.

GWEN G. MORGAN is Coordinator of the Advanced Management seminars for Day Care Directors at Wheelock College in Boston, and consultant to a number of national day care studies. She was for three years Day Care Planner for the Massachusetts Office for Planning and Program Coordination, and the State 4-C Director. Before that she conceived, planned, and began the industry-related day care program at KLH in Cambridge, and is now a Vice-President of the Day Care and Child Development Council of America.

MILA PASCUAL is a native of the Philippines and a former elementary school teacher and guidance counselor there. Since 1967, she has taught in elementary schools and day care centers in San Francisco, and is now working toward a graduate degree in early childhood development.

LOTTIE ROSEN is coordinator of The Early Growth Center, responsible for program development, staff training, inservice development and administration. She worked previously with the Berkeley Schools as Coordinator of Special Education, and as Director of the Berkeley Nursery School for Retarded Children. Ms. Rosen has extensive experience with both normal and disabled children.

DANIEL SAFRAN is a trainer and parent/community organizer. Just before coming to California, he served as the

Director of Teacher Education in the Peace Corps in Kenya, East Africa. He has also served as consultant to the federal government for Head Start, NIMH, the Community Action Program of the Office of Economic Opportunity, VISTA, and most recently for the Office of Child Development. He created the Publication *Apple Pie* and the Center for the Study of Parent Involvement.

PATRICIA SIEGEL is Executive Director of the Child Care Switchboard Children's Council which she helped to found six years ago—A Parent of three children, she has been active in community affairs and taught in a variety of day care settings in California. She currently serves on the Governor's Child Development Advisory Committee.

ELSA TEN BROECK has worked as a caseworker for the Pediatric Clinic of the San Francisco General Hospital for the San Francisco Department of Social Services. She served as the Director of the Extended Family Center in San Francisco, a Research and Demonstration Project treating abusive families and offering day care to children and treatment to parents. Ms. Ten Broeck has been a consultant to Urban Research Systems Associates.

OSCAR URIBE, Jr., Ph.D., has been employed by the Early Childhood Education Division of the Far West Laboratory for Educational Research and Development. He holds degrees in psychology, guidance, and counseling from Fresno State College, and a doctorate in education. Dr. Uribe has an extensive background in research and development, and has directed a Day Care–Head Start Program. He holds credentials as a day care supervisor.

JEANNETTE WATSON is Director of the Early Childhood Development Division, Texas Department of Community Affairs, a position she has held since the office was created in 1971. As an advocate for young children, she has been active in a number of organizations and has served as Governor's delegate, Southwest Federal Regional Council's Children and Youth Committee. A graduate of the University of Texas at Austin, Mrs. Watson served for 15 years as director and teacher at the Child Development Center in Austin. She lectures widely on early childhood development and has written several books in the area of religious education as well as articles on teacher training and young children.

E. DOLLIE LYNCH WOLVERTON, program planning specialist with the U.S. Children's Bureau, Department of Health, Education and Welfare, has since 1970 been with the National Day Care Program, Child Welfare Services for Indian and Migrant's Children, Parenting Education for Adolescents, and the Improvement of Child Welfare Services Delivery Systems.

DOCIA ZAVITKOVSKY is currently the Director of the Santa Monica Unified Schools' Children's Centers and Title I Pre-school and Pre-school Education. She is an Instructor in child development at Santa Monica College, California, and is also a member of the Los Angeles County Mental Health Advisory Board. Her experience includes service on the State of California Social Welfare Board Child Care and Industry Task Force, the California Task Force on Early Childhood Education, and the 1970 White House Conference on Children.

Chapter One

SCHOOL-AGE CHILD CARE

Docia Zavitkovsky
Ida M. Bucher

An ever increasing number of school-age children from varied ethnic, racial, and socioeconomic backgrounds need day care services that are not available to them.

In 1962, in an article in *Children* entitled "Public Welfare's Role in Day Care for Children,"[1] Mrs. Randolph Guggenheimer wrote:

> One age group, often ignored by planners of day care programs requires more attention. A large number of mothers go to work when their children enter school, and many of these children are expected to shift for themselves after school until their mothers return from work. Known as the latch-key group because so many of them wear their doorkeys on strings around their necks, these children are expected to be self-sufficient in environments that offer a perfect banquet of danger—from matchbox on the kitchen stove to the delinquent gangs of older boys who hang around on the streets.

In 1972, in the Report of the National Council of Jewish Women, "Windows on Day Care,"[2] the point was made that while the study focused on

> ...the need for day care services for pre-school children, participants in almost every community found a glaring need for before and after-school care for school age children, and one about which very little, if anything, was being done.

In this 10-year span, the crucial need for school-age day care has been recognized by a few people and organizations, but the voice raised has not been strong enough to bring about action that would decrease the magnitude and gravity of the problem.

Extension of the school day to provide high-quality, comprehensive developmental services traditionally has not been seen as the province of the public school—nor for that matter as the province of any one community agency or organization. Consequently, programs have been fragmented and have tended to operate from a narrow point of view that has proliferated rather than diminished problems. From the point of view of the family, the child, and the community itself, there are advantages to considering the neighborhood elementary school as a stable base for a before-and-after school program.

When such a program is considered an essential part of the public school system, there can be a remarkable degree of articulation with the entire school district. Operating under the same organizational system as other branches of the school district program, administrative procedures relating to finance, personnel, legal requirements, attendance accounting, curriculum, health, nutrition, and social services can be coordinated with those of all other divisions of the school district. This promotes continuity between day care and elementary school, and provides the opportunity to eliminate the artificial distinction usually made between in-school and out-of-school experiences. It also facilitates greater communication and interdependence between the school and home, with the school serving as the primary resource center for services needed by families and children.

An example of such an arrangement has been in operation in California since 1943. At that time the California legislature placed Children's Centers (child care) under the administration of the State Department of Education and local school districts, in the belief that they would provide the best opportunity for meeting the children's fundamental growth and development needs, as well as being the community institution accepted by all as the logical location for children's center facilities. The legislature also believed that the school district had the administrative, budgeting, and auditing facilities to assure the most economical expenditure of funds; that the location provided convenient and suitable housing and playground space especially essential for the school-age centers; and that personnel who could assist in organization, supervision, and in-service training of teachers were available.[3]

The Santa Monica Children's Centers include two school-age facilities, serving approximately 140 to 150 children, from 7:00 AM to 6:00 PM, 252 days a year. Ninety-eight percent of the children are from single-parent families, headed usually be a working mother. Broadly stated, the goals of the centers are:

1.   To provide a nurturing, stimulating environment for children needing supervision before and after elementary school and all day during vacation periods;
2.   To provide support and guidance for the parents in their task of bringing up children; and
3.   To serve as a link between the home and the school.

The centers have a balanced program offering much in responsible freedom, independent choice, and self-direction. At the same time, the need for security, affection, and closeness with a small core of caring adults is recognized and provided for. Children are organized into small groups of approximately 18 to 20, based on age and grade in school. Each group has its own teacher and aide who are on hand for the major part of the child's day in the center.

For the school-age child away from home for most of his waking hours, the centers provide the added continuity of a setting in which the people involved in his day overlap and support each other. This environment has positive effects on affective and cognitive learning. As part of the total team, the extended day care staff knows the school's academic program and can structure out-of-school activities that enrich and supplement the in-school program.

Individualization of the program is facilitated by the use of auxiliary personnel. In addition to the head teacher and the group teachers, who are professionals, the school-age centers have improved the adult-to-child ratio by involving work-study students from the early childhood education and recreation department of Santa Monica Community College. Interns from California State University at Northridge are often assigned to the centers for their field work. There is also a solid core of volunteers. These extra adults make it possible for the individual child to have a listening adult who is aware of the child's interests and dreams, and who can help develop them into program realities.

A TYPICAL DAY

The school age center opens at 7:00 AM. As the teacher unlocks the door, there is Phillip with his mother, a nurse's aide at the hospital. Phillip helps the teacher with opening-up chores, feeding the guinea pigs, the rabbit, the fish. As he does this he chats amicably with the teacher and his peers about his experiences at home, the TV show he watched, the homework he found too hard. The teacher listens and talks with him about his experiences. The center is, in a sense, a family—a larger family than most, but still a family in which each member cares about the other.

There is a give-and-take between adults and children and between older children and younger ones.

The milkman arrives with the day's supply of dairy products. Phillip and five other children who have arrived count the left-over milk in the refrigerator, subtract it from the new order, and help the man count out the correct number needed for that day. They have learned that milk must be kept fresh, so they stack the milk in the refrigerator as they talk with each other about their visit to the dairy, where they watched the milk being pasteurized, bottled, and stamped with the date.

A few of Phillip's older friends have now arrived, and the younger children move off to their room. The teacher brings out some flash cards and suddenly the room becomes a math class with two or three sets of children drilling each other. Children thrive and work in settings like this where teachers trust children to manage their own behavior.

Out in the younger room, where the 6- and 7-year-olds are, there is a lotto game going on with the leader a 9-year-old girl who especially likes the role of teacher. One can almost hear the words and tone of her own teacher as she straightens out fights: "Tell him you don't like that, Billy. Then maybe he won't kick your chair anymore."

The teachers, released from the responsibility of direct control, are greeting parents who are bringing in their children. The centers are an extension of the home, not dropping-off places. They are the link between the home and the school, and it is only by knowing families on a personal day-to-day basis, meeting as human beings, not in defined and separate roles that the true basis of trust and interdependence can be established. The child is the beneficiary of an integrated, supportive environment.

By 8:15 AM the center is rapidly filling with children. Besides the multiplication practice, there is a group in the older children's room who are playing the game of "Life." Two children are reading quietly to themselves from books that have been borrowed from the nearby school library. A group of children are sitting talking. Three boys who are being inducted into Cub Scouts are practicing the Cub Scout Creed. Mothers of younger children poke their heads in and congratulate the Cubs and admire their uniforms. The families are close. They share each other's triumphs and joys and help each other in time of trouble. Centers, by design, offer many opportunities for these parents to develop group camaraderie and a sense of belonging.

In the younger children's room the teacher is reading a story to a group of children. Four girls are playing house in the housekeeping corner of the dramatic play area, bountifully supplied with props to support and reinforce the imagination of any elementary school thespian. Through such role playing, children learn what it's like to be a mother, and in such play acting they learn about feelings—the angry ones, the joyous ones, the human ones shared by all of us, children and adults alike.

On the floor, in a corner, the most intricate of block structures is arising, attesting to skill in understanding shape and size. "Get another big one, Joe," shouts one boy. "No, no, we only need one half that size. That's too small, silly. That's the quarter block—get the roof! Get the roof!" The lotto game is still in progress with the 9-year-old teacher still keeping order. Other children are using the headsets in the listening area.

Through all the activity, the teachers move and tell the children when it is time to clean up for school. At 3:30 AM things are back in order, and all but the kindergarten children are off to the big playground to join the children who are arriving from their homes.

There have been some exciting innovations at the kindergarten level at both school-age centers. At the Ocean Park Center, the kindergarten program for center children is conducted right in the center, with a district, credentialed kindergarten teacher from the nearby Washington Elementary School.

At the McKinley Center, the kindergarten children have a playground area of their own, and the center teacher works along with the classroom teachers and all enrolled kindergarten children before school hours. This center teacher is a credentialed kindergarten teacher who offers an enrichment program to all kindergarten children. This enrichment program takes place in the center with both center kindergarten and noncenter kindergarten children participating in mixed groups.

At 9:00 AM, when most of the children go to school, a group of first- second-, and third-graders who do not go to school until 10:00 AM are involved in a variety of activities —washing woodwork, writing stories and baking a cake. Both boys and girls are involved in this practical learning experience, mixing the batter, greasing the pans, and setting the oven. Even the baking is turned into a science experiment as they talk about liquids and solids, expanding and contracting, and the effects of heat and cold.

Some of the children write cards to one of the children who is ill. The teacher helps by sounding out words they can't spell, and sometimes a fourth-grader does the job for the younger ones. The cards finished, three children address and stamp them and mail them at the corner mailbox. The stamp is a new variety and the work study student from the community college talks to the children about his stamp collection and about the hobby of stamp collecting in general. He promises to bring his stamps when he returns from his college classes in the afternoon. There is general excitement among the three about a new idea for a collection.

Often, just such ideas are the start of a real group project as was the foreign lands collection which the "10 o'clockers" worked on. A large map of the world was put up on the wall. Ribbons led to items below to indicate the source country. Signs with information about the country and the item were made by the children. The whole display was turned into a show in which the group members wore costumes from different lands and told about their collection to the rest of the children in the center. Foreign foods were served at snack time. Not only was this project a geography lesson, but there was all the spelling and writing involved in the sign making, the reading practice in the resource books, and the creativity involved in making up speeches for the demonstration. Above all, there was the feeling of self-worth developed by participating in, planning, and carrying out a successful performance.

It's 9:45 AM and almost time for the "10 o'clockers" to go to the elementary school. First there will be a nourishing snack prepared by two of the children. Because most of the children arrived between 7 and 7:30 AM, it has been three and a half hours since breakfast.

The center now turns into a kindergarten annex. Ten or 12 children from the kindergarten classroom, different ones each morning, come to the center for a potpourri of exciting activities. The teacher's forte is language and dramatic play, and this morning she has all manner and shapes of hoses, firehats, and books about fire stations and firemen. The large blocks become a fire engine with a fire chief, hosemen, and all parts assigned. The work study student, or a participating community college student, assists her. There is hammering and sawing as some children try to build their own fire engine out of wood. There is measuring of doweling and figuring out how many wheel pieces each one needs. The hour flies by. When this particular group is back working with their kindergarten class in a more structured way, these concrete experiences give them insight into more abstract symbolic work. The kindergarten enrichment experience is now in its fourth year at this center and is approved and supported by all concerned.

At 11:30 AM the early morning kindergarten teacher is replaced by another teacher who picks up the center kindergarten children at the school and brings them back to the center for a brief outdoor play period. After a hot lunch in the school cafeteria, they return to the center for a quiet time. Some children fall asleep. Others rest quietly on their cots and look at books. The center is quiet until 2:00 PM— the first time since 7:00 AM!

At 2:00 PM the older children, including Phillip, come over from school. Some children, especially in the older group, use this time to do their homework because they can get help from the center teacher.

At 3:00 PM all 65 children are in the center. Another teacher and the center's head teacher have joined the group, so there are four teachers and three assistants now that the total center population is on hand. There is a birthday celebration and the birthday child visits each room and is sung to in each! Birthdays are happy occasions for elementary school children, and it's having friends to share and celebrate it with that matters more than receiving gifts. The sense of belonging to a group, and of being important to it, build into one a feeling of self-worth.

After the snack is cleared away a variety of materials are set out for the children. Indoors there are art experiences such as painting, clay modeling, and puppet making. There are collage materials of all types, plus records, singing, dancing, movement, and instruments. Some children are involved in crafts, such as making belts, pocketbooks, bracelets and even articles of clothing. Other activities are knitting, crocheting, woodworking, soap carving, and model making. In all of these activities there is free choice, and over the year children tend to try their hand at all the different activities. Success in these areas not only gives children good feelings of accomplishment, but also improves motor coordination and artistic skill, and generally involves problem-solving situations which the teachers use effectively to guide growth in decision making.

In addition to these activities, there is always school play, doll play, block building, reading alone or in groups, and games like "Sorry," "Monopoly" and "Scrabble"—all of which involve reading and thinking, giving and taking, winning and losing.

Out on the playground there is the same stimulating, planned environment that we find indoors. There are wheel toys of all sizes, sandboxes, punching bags, skates, baseball, football, and volleyball equipment, jumpropes, hopscotch, and climbing equipment. These outdoor games help develop good motor skills, coordination, and the all important skills of social living. In addition, keeping score demands math competency and motivates children toward accuracy in formal operations. At both centers there are gardens, an especially large one at the Ocean Park Center, where corn, radishes, lettuce, tomatoes, and carrots are growing.

Although there is fluidity to this afternoon program, with children moving from activity to activity, the group teacher is aware of where the children are and what they are doing. They are aware of her, too, for they shout over from the baseball game or come running to her with their questions and problems. The teachers have learned to do three things at once!

By 4:30 PM parents start to pick up their children. Teachers know the families' schedules and remind children that it is getting close to "going home time." They help them get cleaned up and ready, for they appreciate that working parents run on tight schedules. Such thoughtfulness is appreciated by the parents who, in turn, knowing that the center needs supplies, often arrive with discarded paper from the office or sample swatches from the upholstery shop. Some mothers bring news of "happenings" around town that the groups can participate in—a good, free movie at the library, a special ballet class at the local park, or spring vacation swim lessons at the Y.

From 5:15 PM on, the teachers draw together the group. Children begin to clean up the center as the day draws to a close, and begin to get ready for their parents. Stories are read in the two younger groups, but the older children go on with the Spanish lotto game they've been playing for months. It is amazing how much Spanish vocabulary they have learned. A snack, prepared by the head teacher and some of the second-graders, is served. This nutrition satisfies the children's appetites without spoiling their dinner and makes the waiting not quite so long. And so at 6:00 PM a school day in the school-age center ends. It's been busy every minute of the 11 hours.

SUMMER AT THE CENTER

The summer program at the two school-age centers differs from that of the school year because the children spend an additional 4 to 8 hours a day in the centers. It is the philosophy of the school-age centers that, although there all activities carry educational implications, the program should emphasize its recreational aspects. An effort is made in many ways to approximate the atmosphere of a good day camp. Many activities, in addition to the ones already described, are added to the program.

A drop-in visit on Thursday at McKinley finds one whole class absent because they have taken the public bus to the nearby beach. Another group has walked over to the Lincoln pool with their teacher and an assistant to participate in the city of Santa Monica's free swimming lessons. The other older group will take their swimming lessons in the afternoon. A few boys and girls check in in the morning, but are picked up by the local Jewish Community Center Day Camp bus. They have offered "camperships" in each of their six camping sessions to children in the school-age centers. Two other children are members of the YMCA tumbling class. They are taken there by their mothers and come back to the center on the public bus. A great deal of planning and coordination with the YMCA has gone into this plan to give the children an opportunity to test themselves and become responsible for their own behavior—a growing need of middle-years children.

Middle-years children are still tied closely to their family, and for this reason every opportunity is taken to build close ties with parents. Self-concept, emotional stability, and positive attitudes toward society and learning are all learned best from good role models. This program aims to help parents become the best role models they can be.

Contacts with parents are made through individual parent and director, or teachers, social workers, nurse conferences, potluck suppers, late afternoon after-work coffee hours, parent workshops, and group meetings. The staff works with parents and parent representatives so that they know what parents want and need, and so that parents know what is happening in the long hours their children are away from home.

Parents, staff, and children plan together for children to assume more responsibility for after-school activities, such as leaving the center to go to Scouts, or to the Boys' Club, the Y, the Library, or a neighboring park, and then returning to the center at a designated time. The center staff also assists parents in finding and using available community resources, such as the Los Angeles County Health Department, the Family Service Bureau of Santa Monica, Human Resources and Development, and the public libraries.

The family counselors in the school-age centers are employees of the Family Service Bureau of Santa Monica, and their hours of service are contracted by the Santa Monica Children's Centers. They see their role not in terms of ongoing counseling, but as helping parents to vocalize problems to which they can't find solutions, and toward this end they assist the parents in finding an appropriate referral. They work approximately two hours a week at each center, meeting with parents individually or in groups, sometimes on a scheduled basis and sometimes in a social setting, such as coffee hours.

The health program is under the direction of a registered nurse employed four hours per day during the school year and five hours during summer vacation periods. The nurse is supervised by the physician, who is the Director of Health Services for the Santa Monica Unified School District. She works in close coordination with the elementary school nurses, who keep up-to-date health records on file in the school health offices. It is this office that checks on physical exams, dental exams, immunizations, and audiovisual screening. If the need arises the school nurse, center nurse, and head teacher meet with parents.

There is a dental education program at the elementary school, and families are urged to get preventive dental care for their elementary school children. The school nurse and center nurse often cooperate in this effort, with assistance from family counselors when specific referrals are needed.

Audiovisual testing of school-age children is done by the schopl nurse, assisted by the center nurse. Reports on these tests are discussed with the parents when the need arises. It is the. philosophy of the centers that parents are the primary caretakers and that they should be supported in this role. The centers help to refer parents to the child care services they need, and also to assume responsibility for the health problems of their children.

During the summer, when elementary schools are not in session, the center nurse takes over the primary responsibility for health and safety at the centers. She visits the two school-age centers daily, conferring with the staff, observing the children for evidence of poor health, checking safety and sanitation conditions, and keeping an eye on the nutritional quality of the snacks and hot lunches served at the centers.

In these Santa Monica school-age centers, the staff is close to the children, to their families, and to the elementary schools with whom they join in serving the families within the community. Such a close relationship allows the child to spend his day in an integrated setting where the many people with whom he works share common goals and common understandings. Through the pooling of information and closer ties to the home, individualized planning for the education, health, and psychological and social needs of children with working parents has been accomplished.

REFERENCES

1. Guggenheimer, Mrs. Randolph, "Public Welfare's Role in Day Care for Children" *Children,* Vol. 9, No. 3, May/June, 1962, pp. 109–113.
2. Keyserling, Mary D., Windows on day care: a report based on findings of the National Council of Jewish Women. New York. The National Council of Jewish Women, 1972, p. 33.
3. *California program for the care of children of working parents.* Vol. XIII, No. 6. California State Department of Education, August, 1943, pp. 12–13.

Chapter Two

TRAINING HIGH SCHOOL STUDENTS

Francione Lewis

The years ahead will see a growing need for child care personnel. I have been involved in developing methods for training high school students to help meet this need. My experience teaching high school students skills in home-making, child development, and occupational training, by utilizing the responsive Head Start and follow through educational model, has convinced me of the necessity of designing more carefully a curriculum worthy of the high school student's time and attention. The following pages summarize my efforts, which I hope define a direction that I believe is important for this program.

A child development course based on the objectives of the National Commission on Resources for Youth should grow directly out of the students' own experiences; should help them through a concern for others, in this case younger children; should provide insight into their own conflicts and struggles; and should provide a variety of adult models for relationships with children and for other career opportunities.[1]

The issues of concern are understanding and working with young children (basic child development), preschool processes and procedures (preschool teacher training issues), and relating to adults in a work setting (basic vocational education and occupational training). More complex are the more encompassing issues:

1. Using the students' experiences rather than the teachers' agenda as the basis for gathering information.
2. Helping students feel concern about children from the child's point of view, based on the child's needs, the child's stage of development, and the situation the child is in at the moment.
3. Creating experiences through which students can gain insights and develop strategies toward the resolution of some of their own conflicts and struggles.
4. Guiding students to look at the adult models objectively, and then to relate what they see to themselves in terms of how they relate to children, their peers, and their supervisors.
5. Instilling the students with a sense of meaning and relevance, so that the tasks and issues that arise become important enough to enable them to claim ownership of the problems.[2]

It is essential to recognize that the students whom we serve are quite different among themselves. The facilitator of an effective program should focus on each student to strive toward a program which personalizes instruction and values and seeks ways to affirm the differences that students bring to the program.

To meet the project objectives of the child development course, it seems necessary to extend the curriculum objectives (basic child development, preschool, and occupational training) to incorporate some process issues. I believe that some of the processes which provide meaningful, personalized experiences for young children can be transferred to the learning environment of the youth. No

better opportunity exists than with students who are working in children's centers and early elementary classrooms
where some of these processes are being used.

The children usually move from interest center to interest center as they wish, going from large groups, to small
groups, to individual activities. The choices of activity vary
according to degree of difficulty and in the approach to
building concepts. For example, the concept of quantity
appears in counting games and also in measuring during
cooking. Also, the different activities facilitate learning
through the different senses—sight, hearing, and manipu-
lation.

We start with the basic principle that the teacher can
structure the learning environment (the interest centers) to
expose the children to the same basic skills and concepts
regardless of their choice of activity. The teacher then var-
ies her role in the class in a number of ways. She may leave
some children free to initiate their own and others' activities. Or she may interact with an individual child or a small
group. Or she may address the whole class in a more structured situation. Often the teacher learns most about each
child's interests, needs, abilities, and learning style by observing quietly and discreetly.

The learning environment thus described provides a
miniature replica of the life circumstances children encounter or will encounter. The experiences afford children an
opportunity to rehearse the affective, physical and interactional problems which confront them daily. They provide
an opportunity for the children to develop intellectually,
socially, emotionally, and physically in a guided atmosphere. Moreover, as with the real world, the learning environment provides of number of choices, within limits, from
which they may select.

This model should also be appropriate for the education of teens. Especially in a program that has as its primary
objectives social and emotional growth—that is, a program
that uses students' experiences—teenagers work cooper-
atively, are constructively concerned, gain insights into

their own struggles and conflicts, and are exposed to alternative parental and career models and intellectual development. In other words, assume responsible decision making roles, work as teachers, and understand their own past and present development. In essence, this program asks teens to understand themselves and others, to wrestle with what they discover, and, if necessary, to modify current behaviors and attitudes.

Too few classrooms provide the opportunity for students to think independently and to put their own solutions to problems immediately to work in practical situations. Too often the classroom experiences of high school students place undue importance on memorization and rote repetition, creating a sterile, unchallenging, and fundamentally futile learning environment.

According to Omar Khayyam Moore and Alan Anderson,[3] societies have historically provided activities (folk models and games of chance, strategy, and intellect) for its children, youth, and adults to practice behaviors and skills they will need in the larger society.[4] People seek out and enjoy these folk models, for they create opportunities to experience modified versions of the joys and pains inherent in the circumstances of everyday life. For example, observe the thrills of delight and the pouting anger of young children in the dramatic play area of a preschool classroom as they rehearse their perceptions of interactions and emotions they've heard and seen.

Moore and Anderson have developed a set of principles, based on theoretical analysis of human culture and an interpretation of the Socialization process, to use as guides for educational environments which focus on the classroom as a practice area for life's issues.

THE PERSPECTIVES PRINCIPLE

The environment that encourages the student to "try on" different roles affords him the opportunity to reinforce his preferred role and to extend his point of view. Traditionally the student finds himself in the *follower-receiver* role of reading, listening, and following directions. The student takes on the *agent* role when he writes papers, presents oral reports, makes something, or guides another person, whether child, peer, or adult. The student assumes the *reciprocal* role when given the opportunity to exchange ideas and work as a team with others. This role takes on new dimensions if the student is encouraged to discover the frame of reference and point of view of the other person with whom he is interacting.[5]

For example, students presented with the opportunity of exploring in depth an attitude they hold, whether verbally or in writing, can, through discussions with others, clarify the distinctions between themselves and others. These distinctions can then form the basis for establishing a sense of self-identity, a crucial challenge of the teenage development stage.[6]

The *referee* perspective encourages the student to view his own acts and those of others in relation to a set of ground rules. Authorities, teachers, and books traditionally set the rules. A far more exciting alternative allows the students to generate their own criteria for measuring their success. Videotapes of the students interacting with children provide an objective distance from which students can evaluate their own performance. Just as everyone is his own best critic, so can he be his own best teacher if given the chance. A nursery school or child center in or near the high school can provide an ideal laboratory for the student to feel his way to the most natural, comfortable, and effective role in dealing with children. This first-hand experience, coming either during the academic year or just before professional placement, can instill self-confidence in the neophyte child-care worker.

The traditional approach to high school education only infrequently encourages the student to take risks, to test the full range of their abilities, and to explore relationships to authority figures. From a fundamental sense of security and trust toward his peers and the teacher, the student freely innovates and tests the boundaries of his individuality. The sensitive teacher can contribute greatly to establishing self-confidence and initiative in the students.

For example, within certain limitations the student should be able to move freely from activities that interest him less or not at all, to activities that interest him more. When privacy allows students to experiment with new skills, psychological and social risks are reduced. Students may feel awkward or pressured when asked to make up stories in front of the class. But if given a tape recorder in a quiet area of the classroom, students have the opportunity to try their ideas alone, before exposing themselves to the implicit criticism of their peers. Gradually the need for rehearsal decreases, and students freely improvise before their eventual charges, the children.

Nongraded classrooms can encourage creativity and focus motivation on the proper goals. If grades are required, however, the teacher should allow student to practice skills until they succeed. For example, in our classroom students were asked to observe children's behavior at some length and in considerable detail, and then were asked to record these observations either verbally or in writing or both. The students who succeeded in presenting cogent descriptions were given choices of tasks utilizing their skill. Other students presented evaluations or summaries rather than the required descriptions. The less successful students were not immediately graded lower, but were given a project to improve their descriptive talents or to clarify the initial problem. This group was given a pad of descriptive, evaluative, and summary statements, from which they were asked to choose the descriptive statement, the one asking to "tell what you saw and heard." Those who selected correctly were asked either to redo the original problem or to describe another event in the classroom. All succeeded after this exercise. At no time were they given low grades or were their efforts demeaned.

THE PRODUCTIVE AND PERSONALIZATION PRINCIPLES

The teacher establishes the classroom agenda, varying in detail from day to day, which establishes the projects on which the students work. The teacher also structures the environment to different degrees by the problems and resources he or she provides.

The approaches to education based on these experiences vary in their educational productivity. For example, teaching a young child to count by rote, when the child has no concrete number concept and cannot know why five precedes ten, is not as productive as encouraging the child to count tangible objects to which he can relate more directly. Number concepts demonstrate their own usefulness to a child when he can do things like setting the proper number of dishes on the table.

The idea of students freely exploring an educational environment often conjures up images of mass chaos, confusion, and uncontrolled circumstances. In actuality, the teacher in the intelligently and sensitively constructed environment who has systematically guided students toward effective and productive use of the interest centers encourages more concentration and involvement from her students, even though the classroom is filled with movement, expressions of celebration and frustration, and continual noises of equipment and people at work. To reach this level of involvement, however, *choices* must be available which encourage the student to explore those experiences that are in keeping with his own life style, learning style (preferred sense mode), interests, and needs, as well as those of others. In addition, the learners may choose to work independently or with other. When the Youth Project students were developing activities that would help children develop skills in communication and self-expression, we provided the following activities:

In the audiovisual center, supplied with two tape recorders and numerous books, students practiced making up their own stories and reading them with expression. A videotape camera enabled students to tape others as they worked for later discussion and evaluation.

The art area included a display of completed artwork about which students expressed their feelings either verbally or in writing, or which they simply described. This helped prepare the students for discussing children's artwork with their creators. A display of poetry in the art area inspired students to interpret the poems in a variety of art media.

The language skills area included several books suggesting projects for developing language skills. The teacher also arranged other projects, which changed periodically. For example, she might say, "You are a carrot. You are in the ground. Describe how you get yourself out and what happens to you."

The manipulative toy area suggested a number of games the students might use in teaching concepts like big–small, hot–cold, and fast–slow, and the students were encouraged to act out these concepts through story telling, quiz games, and pantomime.

The music and movement area suggested singing, finger plays, puppets, and pantomime.

Each of these experiences had the same broad objective, but the variety provided encompassed a range of interest and styles.

For the student to make interconnected discoveries, he must be able to use the results of one discovery in making the next discovery. The observation/descriptive statement activity (described earlier) is an example of this process.

According to Moore and Anderson, the reflective part of the personalization principle defines the difference between individualizing and personalizing instruction. In the former, the teacher may prescribe lessons for each student based on needs identified by the teacher. In the latter experience, the learner develops historical knowledge of himself and his career as a student. For example, as the student takes the different roles of perspectives, he is encouraged to see them as different aspects of his own personality system. The authors encourage using the videotape equipment to help the learner see himself.[7] They recommend an experience in which the student selects the portion of the tape which he feels reflects his behavior and personality. Next, independently, others select the portion of the tape which they feel reflect that person. Then they compare notes. A good experience that might evolve would answer such questions as how I see myself, how other see me, and how I would like others to see me. Sports instructors use this vehicle frequently, and we may learn from it too.

SUMMARY

Let me review the initial questions raised and share some possible solutions to these questions.

   1. How can you use the student's experiences rather than the teacher's agenda?

   When an environment is established in which the student has privacy, is free to risk, has a choice, can explore freely, and can identify and work on problems relevant to him by using his own learning style, the student will use his own experiences as he is working with the teacher's broadened objectives. For example, compare the difference between the following teacher objectives: (1) Students write a report on how teachers can help the 3-year-old learn to share from Chapter 13 in the text book. (2) Students complete a project relating to one area of children's needs and describing how an older person can help meet this need.

   The first objective is specific and can be quickly accomplished. The second requires more decision making on the part of the student. Students would have to discover what kinds of needs children have. We based them on my student's own needs. Then they had to determine which resource(s) they wanted to use. They used books, texts, and pocketbooks; they interviewed parents and teachers, and observed children. Also, they had to decide how they wanted to report the information. Most made written reports. Some prepared recorded talks about what they discovered. One student turned in photographs. Reports could have been illustrated, or presented dramatically or as dance. In addition, students were asked to make a commitment describing what they wanted to do and how they wanted to do it. It took lots of time, the results were quite different, and the students were involved!

2. How can you help students feel concern about young children from the child's point of view?

If the classroom environment encourages students to trust their own experiences ("I like people to let me alone when I'm doing something"), and to use them as well as the experiences of others (for another point of view), the students are more likely to assimilate some of the fundamental child development concepts. Moreover, when teachers encourage students to express their differences, they are more likely to value and respect the difference in others, whether children or adults.

3. How can you use the student's concern about children to gain insight into his or her own conflicts and struggles?

The teacher must become knowledgeable about the student, his family, and community to facilitate a transition between what he is and what he is learning and experiencing. Then she can guide the student toward making interconnected discoveries by helping the student take a reflective view of himself and an objective view of those about him.

4. How can you help the student look at adult models objectively?

As students begin to compare the differences between

objective observation and evaluation as they watch young children, as they consider the differing points of view and frames of reference among themselves, and as they compare the attitudes and behavior of various adult models (professional, teacher and supervisor, nonprofessional and parents), they begin to try on the various roles that appeal to them and to predict the demands made on them while working with young children and in everyday life.

My personal experience with instructing high school students in relating to the needs of young children has demonstrated that a congenial yet thoroughly structured classroom setting, in which students freely and at their own pace seek the answers to their own problems, most successfully engages their interest and energy. The classes proceed best when my teaching objectives for the experiences students bring to class have been broad enough to focus on the process as well as the curriculum.

The best way to supply enthusiastic and useful high school students and graduates to the various child-care projects is to relate their educational experience as closely as possible to the experiences they will attempt to create for the children in their care. This requires a departure from traditional high school teaching methods, but the freshness of the experience best prepares the students for the fresh young spirits they encounter in children's centers and nursery schools.

NOTES

1. See "Planning Classroom Activities," Inservice Teacher Training Using the Responsive Program. General Learning Corporation, Princeton, New Jersey, p. 127. 1974.
2. Op. cit., p. 67.
3. See Moore, O. H. K. & Anderson, A. R. Some principles for the design of clarifying educational environ-

ments, In *Handbook of Socialization Theory and Research* (David Gaslin, Ed.), Chicago, Rand McNally Co., 1969.

4. Games such as puzzles provide physical problems, games of chance provide affective problems, and games of strategy provide interactional problems.

5. The film "The Eye of the Beholder" (Steward Reynolds Production) helps students to move in this direction.

6. Erickson, E. *Childhood and Society.* New York, W. W. Norton, 1950.

7. The videotape equipment seems to have so many daily uses in this project that it would make sense if each program had one of its own to use as students wished.

Chapter Three

TRAINING CHILD CARE PERSONNEL

Lucille Gold

Congratulations! You are about to start a new career in child care. You love children and want to work with them in partnership with their parents. You know you're needed, because many mothers need to work or study. What can a community do to help you do a good job? How can we tell you that your work is significant and that the society is grateful to you for your contribution?

We can give you respect, status, and financial reward. These rewards are still lacking in most communities, because caring for children has been traditionally viewed as a custodial, baby-sitting function. Only in recent years has it become widely accepted that a child's daily experiences of growing and living are crucial to his or her maximum development. Each day that falls short in positive physical, emotional, social, and intellectual experiences is an opportunity forever lost.

We can tell you about the knowledge and skills that you will need in your work and provide you with the opportunities to acquire them. That is the purpose of this chapter.

There are four major areas to be explored in training day care personnel. They involve pursuing answers to the following questions: (1) Who are you? (2) What do you do? (3) What do you need to know? (4) How do you learn what you need to know? We will try to expand on each of these areas with some specifics and some references. Each could be the core of a single course, or all could be covered in an overview course.

WHO ARE YOU?

You are a product of your own personal, unique childhood. Your early experiences have contributed to your attitudes, ideas, and behavior as an adult. You are also a product of the times. You reflect the cultural mores of your past and your present. Sometimes these social influences are in conflict with your inner self, and they inhibit you from developing firm commitments to specific values and techniques. You are a continuously growing person who wants to contribute to the growth of others. You are a person in search of a career that will satisfy some of your needs, while simultaneously satisfying the needs of others. You enjoy nurturing and teaching. You enjoy the responsiveness and enthusiasm of children.

The quality of any human service reflects the person of the provider. Therefore it is essential that people who care for children develop a clear understanding of themselves. How does one do this? Group interaction in a trusting, respectful atmosphere allows for sincere, meaningful introspection. When people reveal themselves to their peers, they clarify their own selves, and at the same time see their images reflected back to them from those who listen. This can be an exciting as well as a painful exercise, and it requires sensitive, supportive leadership. Questions related to childhood, parenting, authority, control, attitudes, values, and goals are deeply personal. They need to be examined, evaluated, accepted, rejected, or altered. This is a process that takes time, effort, and patience. It is the foundation of training.

Group viewing of films such as "Preface to a Life," "Roots of Happiness," and "Johnny Lingo," is a comfortable starting point for exploring who are you. The content of these films helps the thoughtful viewer to focus on childhood and parent-child relationships in different cultural settings. It is easier to discuss situations that do not relate directly to members of the group.

When a study group is ready to address itself to the individual members and their private selves, often it is helpful to design a tool for self-reflection—a checklist of thought-provoking questions. This sets limits to the exploration while giving each person the same direction to his or her thinking. It is important for the individual to know how she or he perceives childhood, the role of adults in relation to children, and why she or he has chosen to be a child care worker, what satisfactions are expected from the job, and what feelings one has about parents who leave children with others for care. A sample checklist can be found in Appendix B at the end of this book, but frequently it is better for the group to think through and design its own.

WHAT DO YOU DO?

You wipe noses, rub hurt places, provide a lap, listen, tell, caution, explain, protect, stimulate, interpret. In short, you are a partner in parenting, a teacher, a friend, and a model. You are the most significant influence on a young child by virtue of the quantity and quality of your time and effort. You provide a source of security and continuity to the child's early years. This is a tremendous job, and an important and difficult one.

Although children call you "momma," you are not that. It is vital that both parent and child know that you recognize the limits of your role. Parents are uneasy about entrusting their children to others whom they do not know intimately. They worry about safety, and they worry about attitudes and messages that could threaten their image to their child. They need your services, but they do not want to be replaced. They do not want you to give or receive more love in the relationship with their child than they experience. They want to be sure that you will reinforce the values and attitudes that they hold. They want you to be a *partner,* not a substitute parent.

When you start your work day, you take over where the parent has left off. Your eyes, ears and hands offer tender, loving care. You anticipate danger, protect from pain, caress with affection and approval and interpret the world. You communicate the message, "I care about you. You are an important person." You are helping the child develop good self-images by being a positive, self-enhancing mirror.

Tender, loving care is essential, but only the beginning. You also must use your analytical judgmental skills. You must know what the parent feels and wants, and expand it to the outer limits of your ability. You must understand what the child is doing, how to enhance his/her growth in all its aspects, how to stimulate his/her thinking and exploring, so that each day enriches his/her life in some small way. You must give careful thought to planning for each child's needs, personal rhythm and individual differences. You must understand why one child asks for tighter limits than another, why one prefers to sit and watch while another jumps right in. The degree to which you can stimulate each child's fullest potential is what makes the difference between custodial baby-sitting and professional child care work. It makes the difference in how the community recognizes the status of your job. It requires training.

WHAT DO YOU NEED TO KNOW?

You need to have information about children's growth and development, and then to develop skills to use this knowledge. Knowing about little people helps us to understand

and accept their needs, wants, and behavior. Mastering the skill of coping with little people helps them to flourish and develop their natural potential.

You need to have knowledge and skills in many areas.

About Parents.   Remember that you are a partner with parents. Together, you plan the events of a child's day, giving and taking cues from each other, so that they have sequence and meaning. This calls for general agreement about the child you are both concerned with, the expectations and goals for the child, and insights into the child's uniqueness. A child is secure when there is continuity, not conflict between his significant influences. His cultural heritage, his family's values, his familial patterns need consistent reinforcement and sensitive interpretation.

All parents, including the most distracted and pressured, are deeply concerned about their children. Each generation hopes that the lives of its young will be an improvement over its own. Communication with parents is crucial to establish the trust and confidence necessary to permit a mother or father to leave a child with you each day. They need to feel confortable that you will not replace them in their relationship with their child. They need to be assured that brief, quality experiences which they can offer are as significant as the quantity of time and effort you provide. Together, you make a team dedicated to enhancing the life of their child.

About Children.   The generalities that describe all children involve their need for love, comfort, understanding, acceptance, and protection. The specific qualities of individual children are the things that require study. Variations and differences pose the challenge to child care workers. There are almost as many exceptions as rules, and there are as many ways of reaching a child as there are children. It is like learning the basics of sewing, and then having to create a new pattern for each item. Size, age, place in the family, parent relationships, personality, physical, emotional, and intellectual characteristics all determine the pattern of your care giving. There is no way to work with so complex a person as a child.

Fortunately there is good material describing profiles of the normal child. It tells us approximately what to expect in physical growth, social and emotional maturity, intellectual potential, and general behavior in children at each age and stage of development. A sample of this kind of description can be found in Appendix B at the end of this book. However, you might wonder, "Where is this normal child?" There are so many variations and exceptions, so many subtle differences in children, that charts and profiles are merely a frame rather than the whole picture. Your job involves filling in the individual pictures for each individual child. You need to ponder questions like, "Why can't he sit still at four years of age?" or "Why doesn't she talk when she knows how?" There are no easy answers, and there will be hundreds of such questions.

The skills you need to feel a sense of success with children are varied. Some are learned, others are part of your personality. Patience and perseverance are prerequisites. You need both before you start. Then you are ready to learn through training the skill of communication—the language that children understand and respond to. Positive suggestions, clear expressions or expectations and limits, simple and direct instructions, and thought stimulants become a special vocabulary essential to your work. It is like learning a new language, which requires study, practice, and repetition.

The skill of matching your particular teaching techniques to your knowledge of how a child learns is a necessity. The most outstanding teacher of high school students could be at a total loss in your day care facility. Young children learn through involvement and activity. Self-discovery resulting from a well-planned environment provides more meaningful learning opportunities than verbal teaching. Children need concrete experiences with dimensional objects. They learn with their bodies and all their senses. They learn when they are ready. Adults need to ask "Why?" and "How?" as often as children do. A child appreciates the stimulation and respect that is implied by the question, "What do you think?" The secret of success in teaching the young involves careful planning of the work and play setting, so that the child is exposed to and learns through direct experiences that have meaning at each child's individual stage of growth.

Since you have such a significant role in the child's life because of the time you spend together, parents will hope that you encourage the development of some basic attitudes and values. Consideration, responsibility, honesty, and respecting the needs and differences of other people are all an integral part of your contribution to the growing child. When your behavior and your relationship with children reflect that these are your values, you are teaching them in the most effective way—you are a living model. Imitation is the most natural way to learn.

About Nutrition.   You are not a dietician, but you need to know about the fundamentals of good nutrition. It has been said that we are what we eat, and there is no doubt that children's behavior and health is significantly affected by their diet. Studies show that undernourished children are not able to concentrate and apply themselves to intellectual stimulation. Insufficient protein can reduce energy and motivation. Insufficient calcium can affect motor coordination. Insufficient vitamins can reduce resistance to infection. The obese child feels socially uncomfortable and physically awkward. Therefore it is important that you be aware of the foods you serve to the children in your care. It is also important to plan for eating as a social experience. Food is neither a punishment nor a reward. It is a necessary, pleasurable part of a daily routine.

About Your Community. Include the community in your partnership with parents. Many communities provide services to meet human needs such as recreation, guidance and counseling, health and training. Know about and use these resources for yourself, your children, and their parents. You are the bridge between the families and the community. Put them in touch with each other by your own example and by suggestion. Plan to use all the appropriate recreation facilities as an integral part of your daily program. Invite mental health and medical services to assist you when you are faced with a problem with a child or family. Refer parents to the specific community services that you feel would meet their needs. Your attitude based on information and experience will encourage and motivate families to utilize resources that might help them as people and parents.

About Society. Our country is often described as a melting pot of ethnic and cultural backgrounds. We are a people of many traditions, attitudes, and patterns. However, during our history of 200 years, the differences have not really melted. Today the trend is to retain and reinforce these differences by recognizing and respecting them. Therefore it is necessary to understand the ethnic and cultural characteristics of your children. When you know why a Mexican-American child does not look at you directly, you will not misinterpret his downcast eyes as rudeness or indifference. When you care for a black child, you need to acknowledge that his skin contributes to his beauty as a person, instead of pretending that it is not part of his uniqueness. Child-rearing patterns vary from family to family in any ethnic group, and they vary between groups as well. You have the privilege of activating social awareness and social change to a new generation. You must have the information and skills to be able to do this.

HOW YOU LEARN WHAT YOU NEED TO KNOW

Your motivation sets the stage for all your efforts. "Wanting to" and "trying to" combined facilitate learning. Theoretical knowledge through course work and reading is an essential foundation, but it must be translated into reality by doing. You must experience through trial and error the application of information and skills. There are no neat little boxes in which children or situations fit a given rule. Learning is a continuous process that never ends. There are many avenues by which you pursue your personal and professional growth.

Group Learning.   Many community colleges and other educational institutions offer courses in early childhood training. The curriculum usually covers the study of developmental characteristics of the growing child, educational material appropriate to the young child, psychological insights into human behavior, specific skills related to teaching, nutrition, and health, and the study of family problems and needs. These courses are also available through extension and television arrangements.

On-the-job staff meetings are an excellent approach to continuous learning in a group setting. These meetings complement your college courses, since they relate directly to your work. Some of your specific needs can be met by your coworkers and supervisors, if meetings are well planned and regularly scheduled. Every community has resource people available to assist and consult, who can provide leadership to meet individual requirements. Staff discussions are essential to a quality program, because they allow for cooperative input and continuity on a mutual basis. Two heads are always better than one, and the more heads the better.

Workshops and training conferences sponsored by

professional organizations involved in the education and care of young children are an excellent avenue for self-growth. They provide opportunities to meet with peers from other geographical areas and programs, and they are a stimulating social experience. Membership in the National Association for the Education of Young Children and the Day Care and Child Development Council of America include monthly journals with relevant material, as well as excellent publications for reading and resource.

Individual Learning.   Reading is probably the most basic source of learning. There is a tremendous amount of literature on child growth and development, covering every aspect of the subject. A brief bibliography follows this article, but it only scratches the surface of what is available.

Observation is another source of learning. Concentrated observations of children and those who work with them help to translate the written word into meaningful reality. Question what you see and hear, so that you can come to your own conclusions. Analyze what you have observed, so that you can evaluate your reactions. Teaching and learning are very personal skills, and you need to develop your own style to be comfortable and effective.

Involvement Learning.   The most dramatic learning takes place when you are actually working. Trial and error are great teachers, if you have the courage to try and the honesty to recognize error. Mistakes are valid only when they have taught us that change is indicated. Learning by doing has always been an effective method, and children will tell you very quickly whether you are doing well by them. Respond to their messages and your trials will not have that many errors.

As a partner to parents, you have a great contribution to make. Your work will enhance the lives of others as well as your own. You will teach, love, and learn, as the children you care for learn, love, and teach you in return.

Chapter Four

PLAY IN THE CHILD CARE CENTER

Carol Hardgrove

What do the children do all day besides "just play" is what Mrs. Jones wants to know when she comes to look over the day care center with the idea of enrolling Nancy. Mrs. Jones wants Nancy to learn. She wants her to get a good start. And she worries that Nancy might fool around, flitting from one attractive but meaningless time filler to another. Shouldn't she have to sit quietly and pay attention to an adult who teaches about things like shapes, ABCs and numbers? Shouldn't she memorize nursery rhymes, and use a workbook? Is it too soon for Nancy to be taught that the right to play must be earned by finishing work first? As she watches Nancy get acquainted, Mrs. Jones begins to see more to "just play" than she had thought. Play is not haphazard here, she sees. The children are deeply involved with the materials and with each other. They are, in their play, doing the work of childhood.

ABOUT PLAY

The word *play* is as overworked as the word *love*. Play means different things to different people, and it serves different purposes at different stages of development. To the infant, the toddler, and the preschooler play is the life breath of childhood—the force that carries into experiences of reasoning, relating, rehearsing, and researching. Through play, the child works to understand, to master, to integrate, to try on different roles in fantasy. Children learn through play. They get in touch with new aspects and abilities from within themselves. They learn to imagine, create, develop, and use speech to become more effective; to stick to a task until it is finished; to extend themselves physically, to solve problems, and to increase self-respect. Each accomplishment moves the child toward more challenging tasks.

THE CURRICULUM OF PLAY

Each child is an individual, learning best through self-selected activity and a multisensory approach. Children need to move and feel and hear and smell as well as look and listen. Sitting still on command (being forced to "be quiet and pay attention to the teacher") may make the teacher feel useful, but it robs the children of the real learning that constructive play offers. An adult performance of an organized lesson plan for the under-fives is not the way to help the child learn anything more than how to please that particular adult. There is no evidence that the children's learning centers rest in the seat of their pants. Forced immobility is too often a device that interferes with the kind of activity necessary to form a solid foundation for later academic learning and mature responsiblity.

"Identity is safest," says Erik Erikson, "where it is grounded in activities . . . work, competence and gamesmanship emerge out of the matured ability to play meaningfully" (Erikson, 1974). The child, deprived of opportunities to play meaningfully, is deprived also of the experiences needed to develop later competencies to work meaningfully.

Take the ability to reason, for example. When do adults resort to reasoning? When they encounter a new and unique situation. In reasoning, they draw on previous experiences similar in nature, and in imagination develop an explanation or a course of action. But Nancy can't draw on previous experiences, because she has not had enough experiences to form a pattern that allows her to predict an outcome. She doesn't even have the vocabulary to assign words to the ideas she encounters. Yet everyday Nancy has more unique experiences that demand reasoning than does her father. So what does she do? She plays. Play serves the same function for children as reason does for the adult.

Play for the adult is a refreshing step sideways, an opportunity to gain perspective and momentary relief from the serious business of work. For the child, the play is both the serious business and the refreshing stimulation that pulls and stretches muscles, mind, manners, and mood toward growth. True, children love the sense of doing "real" work—making real bread, hammering with grown-up tools on real wood—but adults who care must remember that the really real work is still the work of play. Adults can spoil learning by inflicting demands more appropriate to their own work standards. Demands for performance, competition or end product can defeat the purpose of play.

With children of this age, what counts is not the product, but the process: discovering muscles and what they can do; discovering words and their magic effect on social relationships; discovering ways of categorizing, solving problems, creating representations of inner pictures and emotions; discovering how things work, like the properties of paints, water, blocks, and dough. Play that feels like work helps the child identify with those powerful, capable adults. Children feel big and strong as they imitate the grown-ups, so long as their efforts are taken seriously, however unidentifiable the end product. But using standards applicable to older children or adults spoils the rehearsal; instead of adding to self-esteem, it brings the child down by pointing out her or his inadequacy and smallness.

Tools that put children closely in touch with their activities are fun and instructional. Lemon squeezers, hand grinders, potato peelers, egg beaters, and slicers are all fun to use innovatively as well as in cooking projects. Even knives and scissors, under good supervision, can be mastered without loss of life or limb. It helps more to teach respect for tools by teaching their correct use, than to preach "don't touch," "too dangerous," and "you're too little." Children, hungry to grow, sneak matches, knives, saws, and other potentially dangerous but thrilling grown-up effects. And using them hastily, stealthily, and ineptly, they have accidents. Wherever a child shows interest, there is the learning edge. This is especially true in a day care center where the child may be otherwise cut off from the homelike but exciting day-to-day adventures of fixing, cooking and responding to everday emergencies with another set of skills. Without attention to these homelike chores, children in day care may be forced to fill their time with boring repetitions of the same child-centered equipment day after day. Putting pegs in holes and rings on a stick has a function, but a child whose daily activity is limited to such experiences is deprived, even though the equipment is expensive and comes in bright red, bright green, and bright orange.

When children are doing "real things," the adult helps them achieve success by letting them do as much or as little as they wish. In some tasks, putting the finishing touches on the project brings a clearer sense of accomplishment and participation to the child than does starting him out at the beginning and, as he loses interest, letting him drift away without a feeling of accomplishment. It is worse still when the adult insists that once the child begins an activity, she or he must see it through to the bitter end almost as a punishment for having begun. Better to sit alongside, show interest and affection, and lend moral support to the child's own desire to complete a project. Children are not always wise enough to choose a project they can complete. The adult can simplify and help them emerge with a feeling of some success, which is necessary if they are to move on to new accomplishments. Incarcerated in a space such as a day care center or a small apartment without materials or companions, a child suffers deprivation. A day without play is a wasted day, and a wasted day in these early years equals a wasted month later. "Sit still and shut up" is the rule that makes a poor day care center into a prison not "better than nothing."

ADVANTAGES OF CHILD CARE CENTER PLAY

For children enrolled in day care centers, most of their play life happens at the center. Ideally, the good things that occur in a loving home can be replicated and expanded in a good center. What might be happening with Nancy at home all day?

Home play often imitates the work of the adults. Mama stirs something in a bowl; Nancy extracts her bowl from her special cupboard under the sink and stirs, too. Nancy and her mother interact companionably and frequently, with Nancy usually initiating the interaction. Nancy asks questions, requests help, decides what she will do. She moves around the familiar terrain, venturing out of range and then returning to Mama. She knows the people and landmarks at home through touch and warmth as well as through sight and sound. If a stranger appears on the scene, Nancy can hide behind her mother or sit on her lap until she checks the person out. She is in her castle.

Although one would say she is playing, careful observation over an eight hour period would show that she spends relatively small amounts of time with commercial or educational toys.

Most of her activities utilize adult-sized furniture and equipment. She cuddles against a soft chair on the rug, or sits on the couch beside her mother for a story or chat.

They eat lunch together at the kitchen counter, and maybe rest together afterward on her parents' big bed.

This environment continually shows Nancy how to be a human being in this culture. She sees how adults work, speak, cope, and take care of people and things. As she watches, she practices using her own style of comprehending through play. From these homely interactions, Nancy learns to value herself, and to solve some of her own problems. She can alternate her requests for help with her insistence on doing for herself. It is not the equipment of Nancy's play that enriches her home life, as much as the atmosphere and the continuing familiar presence of her mother that frees her energy for growth and learning.

Life in the child care center is different. Strange surroundings and unfamiliar adults interrupt Nancy's sense of well-being and inhibit her venturing out. The center staff must carefully consider the kind of nurturing that Nancy and her friends need from the environment of the center so that they benefit from this out-of-home, away-from-mother experience. What makes a nourishing environment?

Nancy spends most of her day at the center, so she needs a place of her own if she is to maintain her sense of being somebody. A nourishing day care environment is one where each child has some retreat for privacy. A second need is for a special adult. Not only must this adult be special to Nancy, but Nancy must be special to the adult. It is not enough to have a number of interchangeable adults who are nice to children; each must have a special attachment or play and development suffer. It is a struggle to keep a child care center from becoming an assembly line process or a child care factory—efficient but dehumanizing.

Special assignments of adults to children in order to form attachments is essential to keeping the day care environment homelike and nurturing. Until Nancy is at home in the center, she relates to her special teacher and uses the other staff members as casual extended family. Her bonds to her special teacher strengthen rather than weaken her affectionate ties to her own parents and family. Although children may adapt to institutions where no such attachment is encouraged, a considerable body of research indicates that such personalities are set adrift and rendered incapable of ever forming deep attachments.

This shallowness of relating, while it may appear unimportant on the surface, and may even seem preferable to the clinging, demanding behavior associated with attachment, has serious consequences to society. People who make no strong commitment to other people assume less responsibility for their behavior. After all, if no one cares, why not do whatever occurs to you? Responsibility for one's actions is rooted in the belief that you matter to someone who would be proud or disappointed in your behavior. Later in life, people internalize the attitudes of the caring adults of their childhood. If at this early age, there is no caring person whose voice one can hear, that sensitive area of growth atrophies.

In addition to satisfying the child's need for a special place and a special person, what kinds of play materials and activities are best?

Given the above-mentioned safeguards, Nancy has advantages that few homes afford. Space, challenging structures for climbing and building, friends to choose among, puppets, puzzles, dress-ups, tools, books, animals, paints and clay, water and dirt are all accessible without the restrictions that such activities demand at home.

More and more, centers are mixing age groupings to make the atmosphere more like that of a family. Children learn by watching slightly older children, and feel their own competence and strength as they compare themselves to those slightly younger. Nancy can watch the older kids cope with situations still too difficult for her and then she can show off her superior skills for younger children. Younger children also call upon Nancy's tender side, allowing her opportunities to develop that aspect of herself. In this way, the day care center offers a substitute set of siblings as well as an extended home and parent setup.

Equipment too allows a developmental mix. Nancy can try her hand at something too hard, complete a task that calls for skills at this current level, and fall back for reassurance and relaxation on something like an easy puzzle, long since mastered.

The work of play calls for good sturdy equipment. Nancy's physical self has a hunger to climb, to push and pull and tug. She and her friends spend long excited periods hauling the large hollow blocks from one side of the yard to another. As they grunt and tug, they shout orders to each other, dramatize their play by assigning important sounding worker-like names to each other: "Over here, Pete. We need a whole bunch more boards on this hole." They must cooperate with each other to maneuver packing boxes and hurdles, tires and wagons, into the desired positions. So that they will get the most from all this physical exercise, their yard offers maximal opportunities for adventure. Instead of a structural steel giraffe that can be climbed on safely by only a few children at a time (and on which the biggest part of the adventure is seeing who can push off whom) there are sturdy wooden multi-level amorphous structures that can be added to and expanded. Now it is a house, now a lookout, now a jail, now a zoo, and now a wharf for fishing, accommodating the comings and goings of several children and groups at a time. The more such structures can be changed about to suit the mood of the day, the more interesting and safe they are, and the more learning they inspire.

Large muscle equipment includes so-called junk materials such as old tires, packing boxes, planks, tree tops, abandoned milk wagons, and rowboats. Everything is carefully checked out for safety. Planks are splinter-free and fitted with cleats which the children learn how to place for maximum security. The doors and glass are removed from the old car; access to slides is gained by climbing a mound or by several wide spaces for climbing up. The traditional playground equipment of the sterile elementary school playground, such as metal slides, merry-go-rounds, heavy swings, teeter-totters, and structural steel climbers are out of place in the day care center yard. They are expensive, dangerous, and do not call forth the learning experiences or physical exercise that the preschool child needs. Even tricycles should take lower priority on the center's shopping list. Instead, packing boxes, wagons, shovels and spades, sand boxes, water play, mounds and tunnels, barrels and boards, blocks and sheds turn the children on to play.

Art activities, indoors and out, vary from day to day, building the children's awareness of their own power and control. At Nancy's age, she's getting acquainted with the nature of paints and clay, experimenting with color and form, but she is not yet ready to focus on making recognizable objects. It is inappropriate to interrupt her learning at this stage by pushing her to "make something that looks like something." Now is the time to reinforce experimentation and enjoyment of the process. Better to say things like "You're using lots of blue, I see," or "You're really working with that clay today." Adults don't have to say "Oh, isn't that pretty" or play guessing games about what the picture or object is "supposed to be." Teachers as well as parents learn to stifle automatic compliments. Who knows—the picture that elicits raptures of "how lovely" may really be about the massacre of a baby-sister.

Involvement in every phase of a project—mixing the fingerpaint, cutting the clay with a wire, passing things, scrubbing tables and easels—all add pleasure and are part of play. If children are involved and encouraged along each step, they may continue to view work as an interesting adjunct to play as they grow older. Too often, adults teach them not to enjoy activities that they otherwise would love by insisting that they *must* do their share of what (to adults) is dirty work, or by taking over and doing all the really interesting things themselves. Mopping may be distasteful to some adults, but it's pure joy to lots of kids. Many a child who doesn't care for fingerpaints enjoys beating up the mixture and serving it to those who do like it.

Crafts in the day care center focus on the homelike too. Sometimes staff members get bored with simple activities aimed at the 2-, 3-, and 4-year-olds. They collect jolly craft ideas partly to keep themselves interested. To the extent that such ideas don't take too much adult preparation time away from the group, and to the extent such ideas are simple and call for creativity and participation from the children, they are fine. Good examples are scrubbing pots, polishing pennies, washing windows, planting seeds, and other messy, homelike projects that call for skills the children possess. Projects that interest adults more than children include those that call for papier-mâché, plaster of paris, and elaborate seasonal cutouts. These take a disproportionate amount of preparation time and are more likely to deprive the children than to enrich them.

LEARNING THROUGH PLAY

A child care center is ideal for teaching health care in the fullest sense of the term. Nutritional information can be integrated as the children work together with teachers, the nurse, or the cook, to add good nutritional sense to the fun of cooking. Preparation for inoculations, for hospitalization, and for regular health care check-ups take place in the doll corner using props and stories to encourage dramatic play. As they watch the children play out their conception of what medical examinations are all about, adults pick up on misconceptions that need correcting. This helps children develop healthy attitudes about their bodies. A day care center is ideal for developing comfortable, nonneurotic attitudes toward physical, racial, cultural and sexual differences among people. Keeping parents in touch with all such aspects of center life provides continuity with the home and community. A good day care center stimulates children intellectually through the use of books, records, and opportunities to listen and be heard. There are more novel situations, more problems to solve, more immediate help to insure success, and more people to watch and tools to use.

For city children, the center allows more physical challenge and daring than a home safely can. Along with the climbing, construction, and carpentry available to the children, the center offers the child and the family such advantages as trips, and excursions to help families venture into the community fires stations, zoos, grocery stores, and libraries. Interesting people can come to them too. Doctors, nurses, policemen, mailmen, all somewhat mysterious and a little frightening in their natural habitats, become friends when they are on the floor with the children on their turf. Children find out that these remote characters are really flesh and blood—maybe even mommies and daddies. As they handle the stethoscope, listen to their friends' hearts, observe the doctor putting on and taking off the dread white coat, they overcome some of their earlier panic related to health care.

SPECIFICS TO BUILD INTO CENTER LIFE

Play in the center would seem to be a natural end product since children here have space, supervision, equipment, and companions. However, the style of these ingredients is important. To provide the proper emotional diet for the early years, centers need to build in coziness, softness, privacy, and time and space for intimacy. Although the center is designed for children with child-sized and child-proof equipment, and with child-centered activities, it is important that homeyness takes precedence over efficiency. Otherwise, there is a danger that the center may become a storehouse for child care. Shiny surfaces of formica, linoleum, plastic, and vinyl need to be relieved by plump couches, rocking chairs, cushions, and variety. The group thrives on variety in height, ability, age, and culture, even among its members. Efficiency can be an enemy to humanism. This is why the center should not include more than 50 children, why opportunities for controlled risk and adventure need to be built into the curriculum and the equipment, and why schedules are flexible and play is free.

The good center environment states its message: "Welcome. Help yourself. We understand you and expect you to be who you are. Here is space for you and your things. This is a child's world, but not an assembly line that you must fit yourself into."

Such messages come across partly through the decor of the center. Art, sometimes children's own, somtimes single object pictures familiar to the children placed at eye level convey the message better than cute caricatures or cartoon figures drawn to intrigue adults.

Mobiles, posters, and three-dimensional wall decorations offer invitations for children to feel, examine, and question.

Because children usually enjoy fooling around with discards and junk, utilizing such materials in the decor of the center invites experimentation. The environment states its message through the materials displayed on the walls as well as on the shelves. The function of coziness and junk is to involve the children and encourage them to use the stimulating materials available to create in their own way. Only as children relate to their environment do they permit themselves to choose and create in their own way.

SENSE OF TRIBE

In a good child care center, the sense of tribe that develops among participating families makes the place an extension of the home and a positive experience for families and staff members alike. It is hard for the nuclear family, often headed by a single parent, to satisfy their own or their childs' need for socialization. When center activities include the whole day care tribe, avenues open that are life-enriching at school and beyond.

Children learn more when exposed to a variety of adults, so long as they have a secure relationship with a few consistent caretakers to return to after venturing out. The little variations of viewpoint and style make life interesting. Values and philosophy are reinforced when shared by many adults. For the only child and the single parent, the child care center offers instant family and instant neighborhood. Families who first meet when their children attend child care centers together often form friendships that last through and beyond those same children's young adult years, and the shared experiences in child rearing are like kinships.

In many homes the parent-child relationship suffers from undiluted, prolonged interaction and irritation. The child care center can lessen some of this irritation by offering other friendly adults and permitting weary parents a break—something that the most loving and involved parents need to maintain their freshness with their children. In addition to the home parent, the center offers other adults for children to turn to, and other spaces where the child may feel welcome. When parents view the center's focus as including and extending the family (rather than substituting for or replacing it), the center may offer more advantages to the child and to the society that the child eventually will take a place in than the suburban tract home or the city apartment where life can be sterile, uninteresting, and unpleasant because of inattention and snapishness from a bored, harassed parent or sitter. Adults tend to become distracted from their children when they do not have adequate challenge and stimulation to interest them in the children's play and delight.

Just as the children need balance in their diet—between homelike activities and educational activities, between privacy and togetherness, between safety and adventure—so do the adults need to balance their activities and preparation between organizaton and spontaneity. But they must remember that for children the value of spontaneity lies in the prepared adult's ability to utilize and extend the play with materials assembled and information at the ready. Otherwise, the children could be in any old environment under the eye of any old adult. The advantage of good child care comes from extending children's physical, intellectual, social, and emotional horizons.

GENERAL CRITERIA FOR EQUIPMENT SELECTION

Some playthings are amorphous, simple, and nonspecific. They can be different things on different days, calling on the children's imagination and ingenuity to bring them to life. Examples of such play equipment are blocks, boards, packing boxes, sand, dirt, clay, water, and paints. Other equipment is self-correcting. There is only one way to "do it right," but the equipment makes the demand. The contract is between the child and the material he or she selects. There are dramatic play props that are sturdy, life-sized, and real: lunch boxes, neckties, and fireman hats, as well as dolls and lace curtains to make into bridal veils.

And plenty of interesting junk stands ready—not tossed together into an unappealing heap, but displayed in such a way that it invites creativity and use. Free access to the outdoors allows children to group themselves according to their interest of the moment. Because they can work on a project that delights them with others who share their enthusiasm, the discipline is easier. Teachers are not trying to herd the reluctant or to limit the involved children as much as they do when the program is chopped into "times" and "projects" that call for everyone to participate or appear to participate in the same thing. Good equipment allows for controlled risk—adventures that permit each child to test his or her own limits without going overboard. The 2-year-old has low platforms and curbs to master; the 4-year-old has a tree trunk with branches to try. Enough challenge is built into the equipment to satisfy the children's need for danger without forcing them to build in extra amounts of pushing and shoving to satisfy their appetite for daring.

Good playthings are amorphous. Their form lends itself to many activities. Blocks can be everything from the toys in Santa's bag to the morning breakfast food. Large blocks and boards encourage the child to seek a friend's assistance to move them to the construction site. Most of the materials in a good child care center demand the involvement of the children in making something of them. Equipment alone doesn't do the job; it is the call to the child's imagination and energy that makes the play equipment educational and body building. Swings and wheel toys should not be the first choice for child care equipment. They separate children, call upon their competitiveness, and offer little challenge to the imagination. When funds are limited, priority should go to those playthings that lend themselves to imaginative play rather than to the endless circling of the yard in the solitary self-absorption that trikes and swings often induce.

Sand and water, gardens and tools, pets and paints, and props for dramatics all are more involving, and they encourage cooperation, learning, and growth. They also call forth more creative interaction from the adults than do swings and trikes.

Safe, smooth wood and stone materials are more soothing and offer more possibilities than does a structural steel apparatus. Teeter-totters and merry-go-rounds are not appropriate playthings.

ROLES OF ADULTS

For play to be flexible, free, and homey, appropriate props must be ready at the right time. This calls for advance organization. If the adults want to watch and listen in order to enrich play situations and catch the teachable moment, they must be there. They can't be flitting about, rounding up and preparing projects or ordering tomorrow's lunch, and still be with the children. For children to have free, spontaneous, meaningful play, adults must plan, make choices, and keep materials orderly and ready for use.

Toys and playthings are bridges to other people and to the child's inner self. They have no other magic powers in and of themselves. Dough is fun to manipulate; so is water. Children learn a lot by using these materials, but how much they continue to learn at the dough table depends in part on the conversation and observations that take place. This is where the presence of the adult focuses attention on color, texture, and the child's power to affect the dough. Is Nancy encouraged to talk to Mary Lou when she wants her tongue blade? What happens when George and Mary Lou mix her red dough with Nancy's blue? The adult enhances the play and makes it become a vehicle for learning, not just an agreeable time filler.

At the water table children are testing objects to discover what sinks and what floats. How much water does it take to fill this container compared to that one? There is much to be learned from using these materials. Just how much depends in part on the teacher.

For some portion of each day, teachers offer planned activities. Some children will enjoy these, some will observe, some will reject. Alternate activities should be available for children with different tastes. By offering alternatives, the message is conveyed that differences in people are fine. Few activities involve the entire group, partly because involving too many children negates the value of the activity. The trick is to have spontaneity without chaos, planned activity without regimentation. No planning results in low interest. Overplanning results in a nonindividualized and sterile curriculum. An emerging curriculum is different from a curriculum that depends entirely on the children for leadership. Between the time the children ask for an activity and the time the adult can get it ready, interest dies. Children are limited in knowing what to ask for when they are not exposed to novelty and variety. Adults need to plan adequately so that they themselves won't become too bored by the monotony of the same play day after day.

SAFEGUARDS AGAINST ASSEMBLY-LINING CHILDREN

Whether or not children "just play" all day depends, in part, on how play is defined. The infant playing peek-a-boo or patty-cake enjoys the play. At the same time she or he works at the serious business of research—discovering object permanency; initiating motor games to elicit a response from the adult; deepening memory paths. What more important tasks could an infant be engaged in?

The toddler defiantly screaming "NO" appears to be doing anything but playing, yet this child is playing with the new and awful knowledge that she or he is a separate being and must develop the ability to affect the world with a puny and primitive repertoire. This is a trying time for them and for the adults around them, but if their activities have many targets for their experiments in encountering the world with its pleasures and its frustrations, life in the world of two becomes more tolerable.

On the other hand, if adults emphasize an activity as a chore rather than as something joyous, the appeal may be washed right out. This is part of the problem of crafts periods in which "we all make tulips out of egg carton cups." Games with rules seriously handed down by the adults, even such simple rules as those for London bridge and looby loo, may prevent play rather than enhance it, because those games meet the developmental needs of older children. Some nursery-school-aged children love them, but usually because they enjoy the adult attention more than the game itself. There are more effective and age-appropriate ways of delivering that attention where and when it is needed than by insisting on a sort of doggie obedience training session under the guise of teaching "drop the handkerchief" or "farmer in the dell." Play energy springs from within the child. Too many orders create a dependency on adult-set patterns, threatening the child's own creativity. Adults in the day care center must beware of the tendency to liven up their own day by using real children as entertainment.

Children need and enjoy the attention of a special adult who is there to admire the height of a climb, the length of a jump, the taste of the pretend pie. From those adults they learn that people are people, not things. They learn how to communicate and cooperate and stand up for themselves. Learning how to play means learning to trust yourself, feel empathy for others, and work things out with others. This, rather than lining up to wait, is the preparation for kindergarten that helps children most. The child who learns to concentrate on his or her own activities has an advantage over the child who must take in all the newness of kindergarten at once: new authority (other than parent), new demands from curriculum and equipment; new distractions. Day care children come to kindergarten ready and expecting to continue the learning that they have been experiencing all along.

SUMMARY

The infant, the toddler, and the preschooler depend on the force of play to pull them toward growth. For them, play is the serious stuff that development feeds on. This is why it is most important for the staff, administration, and parents of a child care center to understand the value and meaning of play for their young charges. If the day care center attempts to become a sort of preschool for kindergarten, or a finishing school to teach etiquette, or a child labor force to complete tasks assigned by adults, it fails the children by depriving them of activities that undergird their later ability to learn, think, act, and work constructively.

The good child care center enhances the home, extends the family, and deepens affectionate bonds by supporting the parents. It adds the play resources of the center to the child and family without competing with or diminishing anyone. Play in the child care center offers instant siblings, instant neighborhood, instant adventure with the comforts of home plus the learning and excitement of the world beyond—in bite-sized doses, self-administered, in safety.

Chapter Five

EDUCATION FOR PARENTHOOD

Dollie Wolverton

Seventy years ago, John Dewey suggested that high schools should train students as teachers by having them work with children in the lower grades. Dewey said that in high schools "the information gained does not find outlet in action. . . . I do not believe any more helpful inspiration could come into any school than the conviction that what is being learned must be so learned that it may be of service in teaching others." Dewey saw how this training would benefit both the adolescent and the young child.

Dewey's ideas have found new life in a nationwide program called Education for Parenthood which was started by HEW's Office of Child Development and Office of Education in the fall of 1972. This program is encouraging public schools and voluntary organizations to offer courses that provide teenagers with instruction in child development and an opportunity to work with young children in preschools, day care facilities, Head Start programs and the elementary grades.

As part of the program, the Office of Child Development and the National Institute of Mental Health awarded grants to the Education Development Center of Cambridge, Massachusetts, to prepare a new work-study curriculum in child development. Called "Exploring Childhood," the curriculum was tested in 234 junior and senior high schools across the country during the 1973–1974 school year. The curriculum materials were used by an additional 331 schools, universities, and community organizations during 1974–1975, and they have been adapted for use by handicapped adolescents and for the training of foster parents, teachers, and child care professionals. The Exploring Childhood materials are now available for nationwide distribution.

To provide schools with information about other approaches to parenthood education, the Office of Education has established a clearinghouse for information about available curricula and materials. The agency is also offering technical assistance to schools, universities, and community organizations to help them design their own parenthood education programs.

The Education for Parenthood program is also fostering parenthood education projects for teenagers outside of the schools. Grants were awarded by the Office of Child Development to seven national voluntary youth-serving organizations, including the Girl Scouts and 4-H, to conduct 29 three-year pilot parenthood education programs in urban and rural areas. In these demonstration projects, teenagers worked as babysitters, companions to handicapped children, aides in child care facilities, and home visitors while they learned about child development, marriage, and family life.

Some of the goals of the Education for Parenthood program are to give teenagers responsible roles in working regularly with young children, to prepare them for parenthood, and to introduce them to careers in teaching and human services. An important assumption underlying the program is that teenagers and young children can learn a great deal from one another.

Teenagers are enthusiastic about having an opportunity to learn about child development firsthand. For example, a student at Cardozo High School in Washington, D.C., said that she liked the Exploring Childhood course, "because you learn from experience. You go over there to the preschool and you find out for yourself instead of the teacher just telling you."

Other students felt very rewarded because they were able to help the preschool children in tangible ways. A teenage boy described a little girl at his field site "who just sat in the corner. By working with her all year, she really came out," he said.

A student at Walt Whitman High School in Bethesda, Maryland, talked about how his work-study child development course had changed his way of thinking: "When you learn how to understand children, it changes your attitude. If you yell at a child, you know that he's just going to be confused."

In the student's opinion, learning to communicate with children was one of the most important aspects of the course. He recounted a conversation that he had had with a 4-year-old that had ended with the little boy announcing, "We're friends now, aren't we?" "That mattered to him! We established something," the student explained.

A senior at Cardozo High who hopes to become a teacher's aide said that what he remembered most from the year-long course was that "children learn by doing. We learned from the kids and they learned from us," he said. "They made me feel I was very important to them."

ENTHUSIASTIC RESPONSE FROM PARENTS

Parents of preschool children are equally enthusiastic about the special benefits of having adolescents work with their children in the classroom.

"The teenagers play more with the children and play at their level," commented a mother of a 4-year-old enrolled in a play school in Minneapolis, Minnesota. The play school is serving as a field site for an Exploring Childhood program in Marshall University High School. "I don't remember how to play with a truck," the mother remarked, "but the teenagers feel comfortable doing that. They're not really teachers but they're not really kids either. They're more like friends."

She went on to say that her son relates well to the teenagers. "I think it's a good thing for him to know that there are people older than he is who are not authority figures." She added that the teenagers "feel very responsible toward the younger kids. They really seem to care about them!"

A grandmother who cares for her granddaughter while her daughter works talked about how the teenagers help with singing, dancing, and crafts at the Lowell Day Nursery in Lowell, Massachusetts. She said that she was "very satisfied" with the teenagers who are working with her granddaughter Jennifer at the school. "They're creative and they're willing," she said.

According to a family day care mother who baby-sits for children in the Lowell nursery after school, "Some of the teenage girls are so involved in the field work that they stay at the nursery school until late in the afternoon. The children need someone who can give them time and attention," she remarked, "and the teenagers can give just that."

In Seattle, Washington, a former teacher described the preschool program that her 4-year-old grandson attends as "good for both the teenagers and the young children. So many teenagers don't have very young children in their families," she said. "It's wonderful for him because the only contact he has with teenagers is the contact he has at the preschool. He'll never have a big brother or sister."

The grandmother cares for the boy while his parents, both teachers, work. "We chose the program again this year," she said, "and I really think that having the teenagers in the classroom was one of the drawing cards. He wanted to be with just one teenage girl last year and with just one teenage boy this year and ignore the teachers, and we have a little problem with that." But she thinks that "the teenagers bring something to the children that perhaps the teacher can't bring to them at that particular age." She thought that the teenagers communicated more at the pre-schoolers' level, and commented, "That teenage girl last year meant so much to him."

The Big Otis Preschool which the boy attends is a child development laboratory school which was established in Seattle's Shorecrest High School when the Exploring Childhood program was organized there in 1973. Another parent of a preschooler in the Otis lab school said that the six teenagers on the rotating teaching teams "plan all of the week's activities for the preschool children" under the supervision of the preschool teacher. The Otis preschool may be a little unusual in that respect. In some Exploring Childhood field sites, teenagers play more of a helper role, assisting the teacher and working with individual children who may need special attention.

THE EXPLORING CHILDHOOD PROGRAM

The new curriculum, intended for teenage boys and girls in grades 7 through 12, including school-age parents, is being offered under several disciplines, including home economics, family living, and social science. The 234 schools that field-tested the course during the 1973–1974 school year were required to assure 25% male participation. The importance of involving boys in family life and child development courses has been a major emphasis of HEW's Education for Parenthood program.

Some of the schools involved in the Exploring Childhood program have set up child development laboratories within the school. Others send students out into the community to work in preschools, parent cooperatives, Head

Start programs, day care facilities, and elementary schools. Some schools are working with children in need of special attention, including emotionally and physically handicapped children. Students walk to the field sites, take public transportation, or drive themselves if they have licenses and permission from parents. An Exploring Childhood manual, called "Organizing the Program," offers practical advice to school administrators, teachers, and parents on field site selection, program financing, legal issues, and arranging schedules and transportation.

Students enrolled in Exploring Childhood spend about a month preparing for their field work by learning about preschools and about common situations that arise in working with children, and by practicing the activities they'll later share with the children.

After their field work begins, the teenagers learn about the stages of development in children, the capabilities of children at different ages, and the ways in which a child is different from an older person. In a fascinating unit on children's art, students discover that children's drawings provide evidence of a child's age, motor coordination, and feelings about himself and other people. Other booklets introduce students to the theories of a variety of child development scholars. The diversity in the theories presented is intended to illustrate that experts as well as parents and students differ in their ideas about human development. The teenagers also practice observing children and consider the whole question of discipline.

During the second half of the year, students study the family and the social forces that influence the lives of children. Documentary films, showing children in day-to-day situations with their families, introduce students to the child-rearing practices of different racial and ethnic groups. Students consider stresses on families and the ways that society meets, or fails to meet, the needs of children. The teenagers are also exposed to child-rearing practices in other countries.

The Exploring Childhood curriculum attempts to build on a student's own observations, experience, and knowledge to increase his understanding of children. For example, students experiment by drawing with an eye dropper on a blotter to gain a real understanding of what it is like for a child to master a new skill. In another activity they set up a play store and ask children of different ages to select birthday gifts for their parents. This exercise introduces students to the concept of egocentrism and gives them insight into the child's ability at different ages to understand what another person might want or like. Through similar activities, readings, films, and audio cassettes, students gradually build an understanding of a child's view of the world.

The course does not teach set rules for working with children. According to the curriculum designers, "learning to understand a child rather than learning specific techniques is more likely to foster flexibility in response to children—a response that will make sense to a particular child in a particular situation."

TEACHER EDUCATION AND PARENT PARTICIPATION

Teacher education is an important part of the Exploring Childhood program. Teachers receive detailed teaching manuals for each unit of the curriculum. School administrators are encouraged to give high school and preschool teachers free time to discuss the goals and problems in the course.

During the national field testing, 235 classroom teachers and 485 field sites teachers participated in 240 teacher seminars conducted by regional field coordinators for the Exploring Childhood program from the Education Development Center in Cambridge, Massachusetts. Teachers shared their experiences and discussed teaching techniques, child and adolescent development, and ways to involve parents and the community in the program.

The Education Development Center has developed a community-based leadership model as one means of assuring continued support in the future for teachers and parents involved in the Exploring Childhood program. In the community-based leadership program, teachers and parents with previous experience in the Exploring Childhood course conducted workshops in their areas for new Exploring Childhood teachers and parents.

This model was tested in seven major cities across the country during the 1974–1975 school year. In some instances, Exploring Childhood teachers led seminars for new preschool and high school teachers on such topics as the roles of the adolescent in the classroom, techniques for using the curriculum materials, and problems encountered in teaching the course. In other cases, parents with prior experience in the program organized workshops for new parents to introduce them to the goals of the course and the curriculum materials. Many of the parents of the preschoolers and teenagers said that they appreciated the opportunity to become familiar with the course and to talk with other parents about child care and child development.

A mother of 12 children conducted seminars for parents of preschoolers and teenagers in the Exploring Childhood program at Marshall University High School in Minneapolis. "Some preschool parents came to find out how the teenagers were being prepared to work with the children," she said. "They were very satisfied with the curriculum materials and pleased that the teenagers were getting an immediate opportunity to put their knowledge to work."

One parent who attended another's seminar said that it was very interesting and productive. "It was really nice," she said, "to talk to people who feel the same way I do and who have the same fears and worries about raising their children. This mother, who has 12 children, said she's surviving and is doing fine!" The parents express the feeling that there should be opportunities at all educational levels for parents to find out what's going on in the classroom.

Education for Parenthood programs that give teenagers experience in working with young children also offer many opportunities for parent and community involvement. In some programs parents come into the classroom to talk about pregnancy, infancy, single parenthood, communal living, and other aspects of family life. Professionals in the community, including social workers, pediatricians, and psychologists, are invited to talk to the teenagers on various subjects. Programs in which teenagers work with young children also offer a unique opportunity for school administrators, teachers, parents, and students to work together as a team.

With the disappearance of the extended family and the reduction in the size of families, teenagers and young children need more opportunities to interact and to learn from one another. Many educators are questioning the practice of rigidly segregating students by age and grade. In his book *Two Worlds of Childhood: U.S. & U.S.S.R.*, the noted child psychologist Urie Bronfenbrenner[1] writes that

> For the preschooler or primary grader, an older child, particularly of the same sex, can be a very influential figure, especially if he is willing to spend time with his younger companion. Except for the occasional anachronism of the one-room school, this potential resource remains almost entirely unexploited in American education. (p. 157)

Like John Dewey, Bronfenbrenner also thinks that teenagers should be encouraged to use their knowledge and to assume more adult and responsible roles in our society. He states in his book that

. . . it is in part the enforced inutility of children in our society that works to produce feelings of alienation, indifference and antagonism. Learning early in life the skills and rewards of service to one's community brings with it the benefits of a more stable and gratifying self-identity. (p. 163)

REFERENCE

1. Bronfenbrenner, Urie, *Two Worlds of Childhood: U.S. & U.S.S.R.* (New York: Russell Sage Foundation, 1970).

Chapter Six

THE BATTERED CHILD

Elsa Ten Broeck

The "battered child syndrome" became acknowledged during the 1950s as a recognizable and treatable entity. Usually, battered—or abused—children are first seen by a doctor or nurse when they are brought for treatment of injuries which range from bruises and burns to multiple bone fractures. Sometimes they are discovered when a parent brings a child to a hospital, well-baby clinic or other facility for examination or treatment unrelated to the nonaccidental injury.

Recognition of the battered child is the first, crucial step in treating child abuse. Medical personnel have to maintain a high index of suspicion about how a child was injured because parents will rarely admit to abuse and children are generally too young or too frightened to tell what happened. When it appears that a child could not have received his or her injury accidentally, the doctor or clinic in all states is required to bring the family to the attention

Reprinted by the U.S. Department of Health, Education and Welfare, Office of Human Development/Office of Child Development, Children's Bureau, from *Children Today*, 3:2, 1974, pp. 2–6.

of the authorities, to obtain protection for the child and rehabilitation for the family.

In 10% of the cases of child abuse, professionals have found that long-term separation of parent and child is the only way to assure the child's physical safety.[1] For the remaining 90%, however, treatment can be offered to help parents understand and redirect the anger that is usually at the base of their abusive behavior and to help them improve their overall care of their children. The treatment is based upon our knowledge of the dynamics that cause adults to strike out against their children.

Child abuse is found in rich families and poor families, in families with one child and in families with many children, in families with one parent and in those where two parents are present. It occurs among all races and economic groups, and among the employed and the unemployed.

But there are some common denominators among cases of child abuse, factors that characterize abusive parents and their family situations. The dynamics that usually set abusive parents apart are the lack of positive parenting they themselves experienced during childhood, their own inaccurate perceptions of the child, social stresses within the family and, often, their belief that physical violence against children is an appropriate disciplinary action.

Most abusive parents were themselves mistreated as children and most never experienced the positive parenting that would help them later to love and nurture a child. As a result, these parents grow up to be deprived, needy adults. As parents whose own needs have not been met and who have seldom been recognized as individuals of worth, they find it difficult and sometimes impossible to tolerate the demands and needs of young children, demands and needs they really do not understand since they tend to view their children, no matter how young, as miniature adults, capable of adult reasoning and behavior.

Expecting that a child will care for them, rather than

the reverse, is one example of how abusive parents share inappropriate expectations of children. Typically, they view their children as a source of love and support for themselves, and, in general, they expect even young infants to be quiet and neat and to hold still on command. When their children are unable to meet these unrealistic demands for mature affection and behavior, the parents became enraged. Their response is violent, as the response of their parents to them so often was.

In general, abuse of children is episodic, occurring at times of turmoil in the household. When parents such as those described above are under stress, the child often becomes the easiest target upon which to release their frustrations. Marital problems, financial problems, and sometimes even so trivial an event as a washing machine breaking down can result in a child being abused. Usually, these stresses are heightened by the isolation and lack of support experienced by most abusive families. Parents often act out against their child because there is nowhere for them to turn to relieve their tension or stress.

HOW CAN SUCH FAMILIES BE HELPED?

> Having experienced some forms of abuse with my own child, having been caught and and having gone through some horrid experiences with the courts and social workers myself, I feel I offer the Center and the parents a great deal . . . (Parent Consultant)

> I try to teach my fellow workers what it is like being on the other side . . . As for the parents I work with, I think that it helps them feel more comfortable with the Center in that they know that someone there has been through their situation and came out okay. (Parent Consultant)

Our project, The Extended Family Center, was established with support from the Office of Child Development in February 1973 as a treatment center for abused children and their parents. Sponsored by the Mission Child Care Consortium, Inc., a Model Cities day care program that serves a multiethnic section of San Francisco, it is funded by OCD as a 3-year research and demonstration project.* It also receives funds from the California State Department of Health and a private foundation, the Zellerbach Family Foundation.

The center is presently serving 25 families who were referred to us because the parents were unable to protect their children from physical harm. Some of the families were referred by the courts and six children are dependents of the court; other families were referred by public health, mental health and social welfare agencies, by the University of California Medical Center, and by private physicians.

Located in the old Mission District of San Francisco, the center has a full-time staff of 14: six staff members work with the parents, five with the children and three are involved in administration. In addition, volunteers and students come in to work with the children on a regular basis.

As indicated by its name, the center's purpose is to develop the resources of an extended family for isolated parents who are acting out through violence against their children. Since one of the most needed services for all the families is relief from 24-hour care of their child, the program includes day care services that give relief to the parents while helping the child.

The center is open from 9 A.M. to 6 P.M. and emergency telephone coverage is provided after hours. During the first phase of the project, when we were serving only 10 families, the children were cared for together, in the day care center on the first floor of our storefront building. (The second floor houses the parents' center rooms and offices.)

The recent acquisition of a second building has enabled us to treat the children in two groups. The original children's area is now an infant center serving children

---

*This demonstration project was successful and much needed, yet it was terminated at the end of the 3 years due to lack of continuation funds. —ED.

under 2½, while the 2½- to 5-year-olds are cared for in the second building around the corner. Separating the older children from the younger ones was advisable since the acting-out behavior of many of the older children was detrimental to the younger ones.

TREATING THE CHILDREN

We have found that all of the children who come to the center need specialized attention. At first, they exhibit behavior that is either very withdrawn or overactive. All are mistrustful of their environment and many are violent in their responses to both staff members and other children. Their mistrust is particularly apparent at nap time and in their fear of such routines as having their diapers changed. All have great difficulty falling asleep and need one-to-one attention to relax and rest.

As a result, the staff's initial involvement with the children consists of helping them gain trust in their environment. Our consistency, lack of pressure, and acceptance of regression help them to do this.

Most of the children in the program go through an initial adjustment period of four to six weeks, during which time their overactive or withdrawn behavior lessens. Limit-setting is particularly important during this period. Abused children have not been exposed to appropriate limits for their age and behavior and they desperately need them to learn how to relate positively to their environment. Thus, how we set limits is one of the most important aspects of our day care program, for it is essential that a positive way be found for these children to learn how to control their behavior. This is difficult because the children usually come from environments that demand unquestioning obedience in a manner that prevents a child from learning how to control himself. Once the children become more trusting (usually from one to six months after their admission to the center) the staff is able to help them utilize skills appropriate to their ages.

At admission, most of the children score below age level on the Denver Developmental Screening Test and the center structures an individual daily program for each child to help strengthen those areas in which he or she is behind. A primary difficulty for the child care staff has been to help these children, who have been continually exposed at home to inappropriate expectations, to develop their potential at their own pace.

We have found that the children, particularly the preschoolers, regress in the center. But once they find that limits do exist they begin to respond to more age-appropriate expectations. With the safety of their environment established, the children are ready to begin to take risks and explore learning with the staff.

Surprisingly, the children have had little difficulty adjusting to the differences between the center and home. Most of them are aware of what behaviors are allowed at the center and what is allowed at home. However, for those who had been most severely battered the discrepancy between home and center has been the greatest and we are watching to see what long-range effect this will have on them. It is our hope that the freedom of the center and the positive support the child receives will help him or her better cope with the limitations at home.

More challenging has been the need to help their parents accept and understand the kind of care offered by the staff. Parents have been particularly concerned, for example, about the lack of physical discipline in the center. Through frequent meetings with individual parents and teachers, and by the formation of a parent board to handle complaints not resolved individually, we have been able to help parents begin to accept and learn from the center's very different type of child care.

The use of day care for treatment of abused children is a new approach both for professionals and parents. As we had expected, in the beginning the parents were ambivalent about this care. On the one hand, they were relieved to be released of the daytime responsibility for their children; on the other hand, they were very threatened by the possible loss of control and/or love of the child. However, as the parents received support from all the staff, they begin to relax and develop relationships with the teaching staff. Parental participation in programs for the children is encouraged and parents have helped paint the center and built play equipment for the yard.

PARENT TREATMENT

I was all right with my little boy but after my little girl came there were two and both children were very active . . . I didn't have anyone to talk to. (A Parent)

The staff is really warm. I was afraid to come here, afraid they'd take my little girl away. But they want to know how you feel. They don't turn you off. They really want to help. People said they would but I didn't believe them at first . . . The hot line here is really terrific for me. (A Parent)

Our philosophy of parent treatment is based upon the belief that the parents themselves, with support from professional workers, are the best source of treatment. Through the use of groups the staff helps parents give support and understanding to each other. Initially, the staff provided most of the direct help and treatment. Gradually, we have seen the parents themselves begin to offer advice, support and resources to each other. Parents often call each other when they are upset with a child or just want someone to talk to. If a parent is resisting treatment, another parent frequently will make contact to help the resistant parent work through his or her difficulty. The parent board meets weekly with staff to discuss problems at the center and all staff members and parents meet once every six weeks to talk over the program and any needed changes.

A vital part of the parent program is the role of the parent consultants—two formerly abusive parents who are employed as full-time staff. Both consultants are mothers who once abused their own children and are now not only able to provide good care to their families but can also act as liaison persons to help develop trust and communication between parents and professional staff. Their participation and openness about their own past abusive' behavior has greatly lessened denial and hostility among the parents enrolled in the program and it has encouraged their cooperation and participation.

All parents are required to participate in four hours of treatment per week at the center. The treatment includes weekly group therapy led by a male social worker and female parent consultant. This group is a formal therapy session during which parents discuss the problems they are dealing with in their family situations. Topics discussed by the group have included marital and financial problems, feelings about children, early childhood experiences of the parents and the parents' abusive acts. The two staff members who lead the group also meet weekly with a consultant trained in transactional analysis, a technique they utilize in their assessment of the group process.

Parents also attend weekly occupational therapy meetings. This form of treatment, generally used with physically or emotionally disabled patients, has been extremely successful with abusive parents. It offers a unique means of assessing each parent's functioning and presents a concrete learning experience for him or her. In addition to these weekly sessions, each parent meets individually with the occupational therapist once every six weeks to discuss her assessment of the parent's work and behavior in the group meetings. Some characteristics of parents' behavior and functioning which the use of craft work as a diagnostic tool have revealed are inability to complete projects, difficulty in relating to authority, unwillingness to try new things and lack of self-confidence or self-esteem. Through their participation in occupational therapy, parents have learned to understand their behavior better.

The center also provides an emergency service for parental support after hours. A 24-hour-a-day, 7-day-a-week emergency phone line is available to the parents and arrangements can be made to care for children and families after hours in emergencies. We have found that the provision of such emergency care has been vital to the center's ability to protect children. Parents have learned that they have a stop gap for pressure that might otherwise have been turned on to the child. Emergency calls have varied from the need to relieve loneliness and boredom to a request to be relieved of the care of a child because the mother was losing control and was afraid she would hurt the baby.

The families served represent a spectrum of abuse— from cases where intervention is needed to prevent injury to the child to cases where a child has been severely injured and extensive work is needed to rehabilitate the family.

Ms. Gomez, age 23, and her 7-month-old child Maria, for example, were referred to the center by a local hospital because the mother had reported to a family health worker that she frequently left Maria alone and was force-feeding her and spanking her when she would not hold still while having her diapers changed. Upon admission to the center, Maria did not sit up or roll over, was very difficult to feed, and screamed constantly. The mother was a lonely proud woman who spoke no English. She was overwhelmed by the change in culture from Puerto Rico, from where she had emigrated several years ago, and she was particularly upset because she was not married to Maria's father.

Ms. Gomez was very responsive to our program. She began attending English classes and became active in the Spanish-speaking parents' group. Through work with a male-female Spanish-speaking social work team, she was able to end her relationship with Maria's father, a married man, and began to develop more positive relationships with men. She also met regularly with the head teacher in the nursery center and began to learn more constructive ways of caring for her baby.

Maria, too, has made progress. Initially, she could only be comforted by rocking in a baby swing. Gradually she allowed staff to hold her and she became more involved in her environment. We found that allowing Maria to eat by herself solved her very difficult feeding problem. With staff support her mother was able to allow Maria to be messy while eating and she even became successful in feeding her.

Solving the feeding problem was a major step in improving the mother-daughter relationship. When allowed on the floor at the center, Maria quickly began to move about and she reached normal developmental milestones in about two months. At the same time, her mother began to take Maria out of her crib more often at home.

Now 18 months old, Maria is a happy, alert baby who is walking and beginning to talk. Her mother is also much happier and relaxed with her child and after 11 months in our center, the Gomez family will soon be graduating. Ms. Gomez plans to go to work and have Maria cared for by a babysitter. The center will help her carry out her plans.

Very different problems are involved in our work with the Smith family, which was referred to us by the Juvenile Court.

Elaine Smith was three months old when she was admitted to a hospital for treatment of fractured jaws, ribs and arms. Neither parent could explain the injuries. The hospital diagnosed Elaine as a battered child; her mother was arrested and placed on probation for child abuse. Elaine was placed with a relative for five months until our center opened. Upon the agreement of the parents and the Juvenile Court to work with the center, Elaine was released to her parents.

After initial resistance Mr. and Mrs. Smith became very involved with the center. They described it to staff as a "home away from home" and a central part of their lives. Both parents are active in the parents' group. Mr. Smith has joined the parent board and frequently helps staff with such jobs as painting, obtaining supplies, manning the telephones and greeting guests.

Elaine was extremely withdrawn when she first came to the center. She would sit and not move unless picked up by a staff member. She would become very anxious and unhappy when she was being dressed or undressed; she would not nap and rarely played with toys. Now, after 11 months in the program, she is gradually beginning to relax and is much more active. She plays easily but is quite violent towards other children, scratching and biting when she is approached.

Elaine has become attached to staff members and is eager to attend the center, but she continues to be very quiet when she is with her parents and usually appears quite fearful in their care.

Despite the Smiths' participation in the program, the staff has been unable to help them solve their primary problem, drug addiction. Through their involvement at the center both parents began to trust the staff enough to be honest about their drug usage and its effect upon their lives. With the help of the teaching staff, the Smiths finally admitted to the negative effects of their drug usage upon Elaine and they are beginning to struggle with the need to involve themselves in a drug treatment program. We have made it clear to both parents that unless they actively cope with their drug problem the center would have to recommend to the Juvenile Court that Elaine be removed from their care.

During the last two months both parents have sought help and Elaine's behavior has improved in the center. Both the Smiths and the staff recognize, however, that help from the center will be needed for a long period of time before Elaine will be totally safe in their home.

A couple whose family problems have been greatly alleviated by their participation in the center are the Goodmans. Both parents in this family have a history of deprivation and abuse in their own childhood. Their two children, Billy, aged 4 and Susan, 1½, were referred to the center by a local hospital because they had suffered many unexplained injuries at home. The family was referred to the Juvenile Court which agreed not to remove the children as long as the family cooperated with the center.

Mr. and Mrs. Goodman quickly indicated to staff members their need for marital counseling. Mrs. Goodman was excessively dependent on her husband and very jealous of the children. Mr. Goodman was also a very dependent person with no idea of how to care for the children and his helpless wife. He responded to the children as his parents had responded to him: expecting a great deal from them and beating the children when they did not respond.

Both parents have found a refuge in the center. Mrs. Goodman comes daily and works on a variety of projects. She is finding that she can be independent and a person of value separate from her husband and children. Mr. Goodman has found supportive help for his frustrations and alternatives on how to handle his anger.

Both children enjoy the center program and are beginning to respond to staff attention. Billy is now speaking and Susan, although very wary, is now playing with other children. The hospital staff had reported at the time of referral that they had never seen the children smile during any of their contacts with them. After three months in the center, both children smile and laugh easily and with enthusiasm.

To augment the more formal aspects of the program, each family is assigned an individual worker who is responsible for coordinating the center services with those provided by other agencies. All workers provide an atmosphere of nurturing and support that gives the parents the emotional resources they need to better care for their children.

This type of service is extremely demanding on staff. Rarely is it formal therapy that brings about changes in the behavior of abusive parents. Rather, we have found that it is the relationships between parents and staff and parents and parents that allow a parent to gradually develop the confidence needed to bring about the necessary change in his or her behavior.

Work with abusive parents requires the ability to give in a very total way to demanding, needy adults. The rewards in this type of work are not typical. Rarely does a worker get thanked or feel that he is directly appreciated by the families. However, the satisfaction of watching parents change and assume positive care of their children is an experience that brings rewards rarely found in any other profession.

REFERENCE

1.   *The Battered Child,* edited by Henry Kempe and Ray Helfer, University of Chicago Press, 1968.

Chapter Seven

THE DISABLED CHILD

Lottie Rosen

Every healthy living organism strives to achieve its potential, to thrive, to grow, to be productive. The young child, unless sick or thwarted, wants to explore, learn, and grow. In this society the home, the school, and the community provide the nourishment and the environment in which our children may thrive and grow or be thwarted, stunted, or even die. Thus it is contingent upon all concerned to provide that quality of nourishment and environment that permits each child to build a strong, healthy body and an exploring, growing, productive mind.

Meeting the physical needs of the body is a relatively straightforward task, with much available specific information and little disagreement. Meeting the developmental needs of the mind presents much greater and more complex problems in the face of a wealth of differing and often conflicting theories. Nearly everyone, however, agrees that the early years of a child's life are crucial to learning, mental development, and the attainment of his or her highest intellectual potential.

The child must have stimulation, encouragement, materials, and guidance to develop and continue the desire to learn. Recognizing this, home, school, and community have worked together toward providing nursery school programs for young children.

The Berkeley Unified School District (BUSD) has operated parent cooperative nursery schools and children's centers (child care) for more than 30 years. These schools have had a flexible admissions policy, and the population of children entering these programs has always included some children with physical, emotional, or learning problems that interfered with their social adjustment or ability to function in school. Despite the concern and efforts of teachers over the years, they often have felt frustrated by their inability to provide appropriate programs and to dispel the confusion of the parents and their fears for the future of their children. After a particularly difficult year, one of the administrators became determined to seek help for these children, their parents, and the teachers.

The Early Growth Center was funded by the Bureau for Education of the Handicapped[1] in 1971. Because the Berkeley schools had been pioneers in supporting early childhood programs, we had the unique opportunity to demonstrate that young handicapped children can participate in regular programs.

Physical handicaps do not always require special facilities. Many children with cerebral palsy, and impairments of speech, hearing, vision, and general health can succeed in regular grade placement when given the needed emotional support and appropriate program planning and parent counseling. Flexible programming can be arranged so that children needing special classes, such as signing for deaf children, can attend special programs for part of the day and learn in the regular class for another part of the day. This is particularly important for children of working parents who need child care services beyond the usual hours of the special class.

Children with developmental problems due to neurological, emotional, or deprivational causes may exhibit behavior and learning problems which may result in placement in educationally handicapped (EH) or educable mentally retarded (EMR) classes. The benefits of the special class—small class size, individualization, and a specially trained staff—are overshadowed for many children by the resultant isolation, which contributes to their inability to function in the world outside their classroom. Relationships with the peer group, lack of isolation, and the more challenging experiences of the regular class can be realized by these children through appropriate intervention at the preschool level.

In most large cities, the population of these special classes are often disproportionately filled with boys of minority cultures. There may be several reasons for this prevalence. In their early years, boys are more active physically and less receptive to formalized learning than girls. Some teachers may not be sensitive to these differences and may perceive the boys as resistant nonlearners who are acting out and need special class placement. Nursery school programs must set their priorities to break this pattern of injustice.

Every school district today finds itself in a constant struggle with problems and issues brought about by rapid social changes and resistance to change. These issues cover the whole range of the philosophy and methodology of education. As you introduce any change in a particular school, all of the strengths and weaknesses and conflicts of that school come into play. If you keep focused on the best interests of all of the children, the reorganization that results will lead to an improved program for the children, the teachers, and the parents.

When a school takes on a commitment to integrate handicapped children and to prevent and minimize handicapping conditions, the staff and administration must take a critical look at itself, the school environment, and the curriculum, and must ask itself some probing questions. Is there consensus on a philosophy and resultant goals that are relevent to the children enrolled? Does the school provide education of high quality to all the children? Is the teaching schedule planned to allow for maximum time and energy to meet the needs of children? Is the school plant being utilized fully?

PHILOSOPHY AND GOALS

Child care programs have been changing from custodial institutions to a blend of home and nursery school embodying the best of both environments with the goal of preparing an independent child with a zest for life, ready to take on his next challenge—school. To achieve a happy blend of home and nursery school, the following features of each should be included:

HOME

1. Security—knowing where things are, what to do with things, who cares for you, the constancy of people and things, a feeling of belonging.
2. Comfort—soft places to sit or lie, privacy or company as needed or wanted, a choice of noisy or quiet places, snacks, warmth, good feelings, an informal relaxed atmosphere.
3. The presence and availability of adults to communicate with, to gain comfort from, to play with, to learn from.
4. Material things—books, toys, TV, records, pets, plants, paper, crayons—each with its place and purpose and its learning and pleasure-giving possibilities.
5. Meeting physical needs—a place to eat, to rest, to sleep, to use the toilet.
6. Love—with its recognition of the child as a special person.
7. A place for the child in a planned, structured scheme of things.

SCHOOL

1. A place to explore and learn about new things.
2. A place for new experiences, creative challenges, and fun.
3. A place to make new friends.
4. A place to meet adults in a new role.
5. A place to experience group structure and to find your place within it.
6. A place to experience socialization—sharing, responsibility, interaction with peers.
7. A place that helps prepare the child to meet the new challenges of life.
8. A place that is orderly, organized, and designed to allow the child to function with a minimum of stress.

To sum up—a happy blend of home and school would provide a child with basic care, nurturance, opportunities for socialization, and education. These elements are provided by the program, the environment, and the teacher.

PROGRAM

Parents and teachers may have differing educational philosophies, from structure versus permissiveness, to teacher-directed learning versus discovery and exploring. Despite these differences, a fruitful approach to program planning would be to seek out the growth needs common to all children. They may find that regardless of racial, ethnic, or economic background, all children should have an opportunity to make their own choices of activity and to follow the routine of structured activity. Each child should learn to function independently and to take direction. The adults involved must plan a balanced program of activities combining the best features of structure and an open plan to make learning a pleasurable experience for the child.

One question that always comes up is how to ensure a child's participation in the activities planned. The child who most needs to develop fine-motor skills or language abilities often tends to avoid these areas. If the adults are convinced that certain experiences are important for children, these activities must be scheduled so that they cannot be avoided. How often do we permit a child to avoid lunch? If we plan nourishment for the mind as well as for the body, then certain activities should occur each day at a set time with a set place for each child. Activity centers to include the development of motor and language skills, as well as thinking and reasoning, should become a vital, structured part of each child's day.

TEACHERS

Teachers in a child care setting are beset with many problems of role identification. Is she or he a surrogate parent, a teacher, a housekeeper, or all three? The child's best interests are served if the role becomes defined as another loving, caring adult in the child's life, responsible for protecting, guiding, and challenging the child. Mothering can become smothering, and overemphasis on housekeeping can siphon off time and energy that can be more advantageously spent. Beds with pads and sheets can be replaced by mats that children can handle themselves. Snacks can be set up for children to help themselves when they are hungry. Art, science, and nature activities should have a place apart from the mainstream, and permanent activity centers should be established. Accomplishing these goals would minimize the fetch-and-carry and cleanup chores. Teachers should be able to choose their areas of interest and be assigned for long periods of time to facilitate planning and continuity. Planning time must be scheduled at least two hours each week to allow teachers to prepare for their areas.

THE SCHOOL PLANT

All possible space should be explored for maximum utilization. Thought should be given to the flow of traffic and to the schedule changes in each day. Children and parents come and go at different times. Can the cubbies be placed in an area that provides easy accessibility and minimum disruption? Children eat, sleep, and play in the same room. Tables, chairs, and activity centers should be arranged to minimize the need for moving things around. Shelves should be arranged so that children can see what is in them, reach things easily, and put them away when finished. Each area of the environment gives obvious messages to children, allowing them to be independent and to develop a sense of pride in their school.

A MODEL DEVELOPMENTAL CHILD CARE PROGRAM

King Children's Center, with a population of 35 children, has become the model program for the Early Growth Center. About 80% of the children come from single-parent families, mostly mothers who are students or employed or both, and who carry a heavy load of responsibility. There are white, black, and Oriental families in the school. Five handicapped children were also introduced into the school —a child with cerebral palsy, an educable mentally retarded child with genetic birth defects, a child with no speech, and two children with developmental problems. All of these children participate in all aspects of the program.

A prone board was designed for the child with cerebral palsy to let her assume a comfortable position during table activities. She receives physical therapy twice a week from a Children's Hospital physical therapist, and 15 minutes daily at school from a teacher trained by the physical therapist. The child with no speech receives speech therapy twice a week from an Early Growth Center staff member, a speech and hearing specialist, and daily tutorial help from a teacher trained by the specialist. The educable mentally retarded child and the children with developmental problems receive tutorial help each day for 15 to 30 minutes from a teacher in consultation with teacher specialists from the Early Growth Center.

The schedule at King was reorganized to provide for activity centers and time for meeting individual needs. All children participate in activity centers. Activity centers are organized so that children have an opportunity to explore and manipulate materials and to deal with their related concepts and language. In the morning these activities are planned and guided by a teacher, and in the afternoon the centers are available for children to practice and explore on their own. One large room with a table and five chairs set in each of the four corners, a set of shelves and a screen for each, provides four activity centers.

Activity centers and language development activities were planned to provide the child with an instructional program in school readiness skills, fine-motor development, prewriting skills, math reasoning, and thinking, reasoning, and problem solving. Children are in close, warm relationships with teachers in groups of four.

Centers are scheduled for four days each week; the fifth day is set aside for trips. All children are called to centers by a pleasant-sounding cow bell. Four-year-olds make their own choice of centers; 3-year-olds are assigned. Children stay at a center for a month and then move to another center. Each child has two or three experiences in each center.

Language development activities are held at the same time in another room. Three teachers are assigned to from 15 to 18 children. The group comes together for songs, finger plays, rhythms, and so on, and then break down into three groups of five to six children for conversational experiences concerned with cooking, science, flannel board materials, stories, and other topics.

PLANNING FOR CENTERS

1. Teacher's tasks in preparing
   A. Identify specific skill or task.
   B. Identify concept.
   C. Plan language to use.
   D. Plan one more challenging step.
   E. Plan one simplifying step.
   F. Prepare materials needed.
   G. Place materials in center on shelves.
2. Teacher's role
   A. Familiarize children with the materials to be used. Explain, let them touch, look, and ask questions.
   B. Demonstrate or model if necessary.
   C. Proceed with activity—take turns with children.
   D. Observe and guide children. Provide more input if needed, and answer questions.
   E. Use observations for further planning.
3. Suggested time
   This time breakdown permits a child with a short attention span to move freely when he needs to, and allows a child who wants to become more involved with a specific task to do so.
   A. 15 minutes—group activity—teacher-directed.
   B. 15 minutes—individual activity—continued use of materials from group activity or choices from the shelves in the center.
   C. 15 minutes—continue free choice in center or move to other centers in the room.

4. Suggested amount of materials in the center each day
   A. Those needed for group activity.
   B. Two additional choices per child on shelves.
   C. Change materials as needed. Keep favorites longer. Think up challenging, infrequently chosen ways to present materials.

MEETING INDIVIDUAL NEEDS

Handicapped children, children who score low on district tests, and children whom teachers feel need special attention for behavior or learning problems are assigned individual time. Activities are planned to provide special help in the school readiness skills—relating to adults or other children or focusing attention on a task. Time is allotted in the morning and afternoon for 15 to 30 minutes of individual or small group activities. Each child's program is individualized to meet his needs and sequenced for progress. Some children need only a closer relationship with an adult in a consistent manner to blossom forth and share what they already know. Children who have experienced failure for whatever reasons need time and nonthreatening situations in order to develop trust in themselves and others.

Activity centers, individual time, lunch, and naps constitute the structured part of the day. During the rest of the day children are free to make their own choices, including the choice of being by themselves and doing "nothing." Every adult reserves some time to be free of other people or activities to maintain his or her peace of mind. We should not deny this right to children; overstimulation can be as harmful as understimulation.

The daily schedule looks like this:

7:30–10:00   Free Play. Children may choose from among different games, manipulative toys, books, block play, outdoor play, and art and science activities. A breakfast snack is available during this time.

9:00–10:00	Time for meeting individual needs.
10:00–10:30	Gross motor activity.
10:30–11:15	Activity center time.

    1. Yellow room: Group language development activity—finger plays, songs, rhythms, stories in a large group. Getting acquainted with materials and conversation in two smaller groups.

    2. Blue room: Four children, with one teacher in four different activity groups:

        A. Fine-motor activities: pegs, beads, construction toys, etc.

        B. Prewriting activities: crayons, felt pens, chalk, scissors, paste, etc.

        C. Math reasoning activities: experiences with quantity, size, shape, measuring, etc.

        D. Thinking, reasoning, and problem solving: experiences with sorting, classifying, associating, and remembering.

11:15–11:30	Getting ready for lunch.
11:30–12:00	Lunch.
12:00–12:15	Stories.
12:15– 2:15	Toileting. Nap time. (The time varies with each child's needs.)
2:15– 3:15	Time for meeting individual needs.
2:30– 5:45	Free play. Children may choose from among playroom activities, art, music, outdoor play, and center activities. "Sesame Street" is shown on TV at 4:30.

IN-SERVICE TRAINING

In-service training is the most important aspect of the Early Growth Center program. A series of lectures, practicum sessions, and workshops covering child development, special problems of young children, and curriculum is provided for all teachers. Specialists and Early Growth Center staff conduct the lectures and workshops. Interns meet with the Early Growth Center coordinator to plan the practicum sessions that they conduct in their schools.

The model school serves as a training center for teachers in the other children's centers and parent nursery programs in the Berkeley Unified School District. Teachers can sign up for internships for one month. Substitute teachers are provided to replace them in their home schools. During this month they observe and participate in all the activities. In the last week of the month, they plan for and supervise one or two activity centers. The interns also visit other special programs and receive training in planning sequenced lessons. Interns work under the supervision of the Early Growth Center Staff, and when they return to their schools, each one plans for some adaptation of the model program. The Early Growth Center provides ongoing technical assistance, and thus each school begins to integrate handicapped children.

NOTE

1. Approximately one million nursery school age children in the United States suffer from a handicap that will prevent them from participating fully in school and society. The extent of unmet needs of children in this age range prompted the enactment of the Handicapped Children's Early Education Assistance Act in 1968. This act provided money for demonstration programs that could serve as models for replication. There are now about 100 programs for young handicapped children throughout the country.

Chapter Eight

THE BLACK CHILD

James A. Johnson, Jr.

After completing this chapter, the reader will be able to:

1. Discuss four reasons why the demand for child development services is increasing in the black community.
2. Discuss three reasons why child development services that are currently being offered to low-income black parents and their children should be assessed.
3. Discuss the mission of child development centers.
4. Discuss the sociocultural nuturing environment of low-income black children.
5. Discuss four reasons why low-income black parents are increasingly required to purchase child development services.
6. Discuss ways in which these services contradict the low-income black child's previous experience.
7. Discuss the consequences of such requirements for the growth and development of low-income black children.

8. Discuss a means for acquiring descriptive information about the nature and needs of low-income black children.
9. Discuss a means for evaluating child development services for low-income black children from the perspective of the parents of those children.

PROBLEMS AND ISSUES

Throughout the nation the demand for child development services is increasing rapidly. There are many reasons for this rapid increase in demand. One of these reasons is the unfortunate position taken by the state of California about parents of dependent children who are receiving state aid. Essentially, this position is that if parents don't work, their children will not eat. This policy has meant that many parents who depend on state aid to feed, house, and clothe their children have been required to go to work on menial, dead-end nonjobs in order to continue receiving the few dollars a month that they receive from social service agencies with which they manage to support their children.

A second reason for the rapidly growing demand for child care services is inflation. According to the most recent estimate of the consumer price index, a family with an income of $7000 in 1967 had a spending power of $4746 in 1974. To keep pace with inflation, more and more women are going to work to supplement their husbands' incomes.

A third contributor to this growing demand is the increasing social and psychological stress on people. This results in parents seeking child development services in order to acquire the option of "coming up for air."

Fourth, the assertions and rhetoric of the early childhood development establishment opinion-makers have coerced growing numbers of parents to enroll their children in preschools increasingly earlier. Typically, these parents have been led to perceive child development services as vehicles for getting their children "ready" for school.

Forced work "programs," supplementing the family income, seeking relief from social and economic stress, and anxiety about how children will fare in school are not all the possible reasons for the growing demand for child development services. However, these reasons do explain why a sizeable portion of low-income black parents are making these demands. Accordingly, it seems justified to assess the child development services now being provided for low-income black children.

Such an assessment is justified on at least three bases. First, the middle-class-oriented child development center, as we know it, is a relatively new institution, and it is an institution that is foreign to indigenous black culture. Second, irrespective of the quantity or quality of child development services that are presently available to low-income parents of black children, the very nature of these services needs examination. Third, incentive systems, rules, and procedures that are rapidly becoming a part of typical child development institutions throughout the nation are often in conflict with what the low-income black child has learned before being exposed to these institutions.

We begin with the assumption that child development centers have two coequal missions: (1) to protect the health and safety of children, and (2) to provide opportunities for children to manipulate the environment more effectively. We find no argument with these missions. However, we are very concerned about how these missions are accomplished.

This is because low-income black children are usually nurtured in what sociologists refer to as "extended families." Extended families are families that include not only parents and children ("nuclear families"), but also include aunts, uncles, cousins, grandparents and great-grandparents, and sometimes even friends. Children who are nurtured in extended families learn that while they are responsible to many adults for their actions, they can depend on this wide ranging network of adults to meet their social, psychological, and emotional needs. Additionally, they interact with a set of children, including siblings and other children in the extended family, who span a wide age range.

Traditionally, child development services in the black community were provided by persons in the extended family. Where this was not possible, the parents would simply choose a person who had earned legitimacy. That is, the parents would select a person who, in their judgment, treated children in ways that were consistent with their own value system. In this chapter we refer to this person as "the lady around the corner."

Because of the increased demands for ladies around the corner, and because of other factors, ladies around the corner are becoming increasingly unable to keep up with the demand for services. Some of these other factors are (1) legislation designed to police and regulate the child development industry; (2) child-development-related public policy; (3) the inflationary cost of child development services; and (4) the growing attitude among the child development establishment that the quality of service provided by the lady around the corner is inadequate. These four factors have resulted in professionalism and certification requirements. This in turn has resulted in the ultimatum that if the lady around the corner does not enter and complete training programs, she will be forced out of business.

In short, the service that many low-income black parents prefer must either "go underground" or become significantly modified, because the lady around the corner who enters training programs will not be certified as "competent" until she can demonstrate that she has been socialized to middle-class Euro-American norms. Being socialized to these norms will mean that she will talk differently, walk differently, be seen frequently in the company of middle-class Euro-Americans, eat what Euro-Americans eat, and, in general, behave in ways that are inconsistent with the ways in which she behaved before training. Certification may even mean that the lady around the corner will move, and this will result in a reduction of the child development services preferred by many low-income parents in the black community.

This condition, in turn, results in the coercion of low-income black parents to place children in situations where they have control over such factors as personnel, policy, budget, program, and management; or to place children in situations in which they have no such control. Given that the former situations are few and far between, low-income black parents in reality have no choice but to place children with persons who are or who imitate middle-class and Euro-American persons.

Black children in child development centers may be looked at, then, as a captive audience, there for many different reasons and socialized to a set of norms, expectations, rules, and incentive systems by the extended family that may conflict with those of child development centers. Their parents may be in a bind because they face the agonizing choice of attending to their children's physical *or* sociocultural needs. In other words, if parents awake their children at 6 AM to drop them off at the center and arrive at work on time, and prepare their children for bed at 7 PM, the only sociocultural contact they may have with their children is kissing them "good-morning" and "good-night."

During the day the children are exposed to persons who (1) view the world through their own cultural "glasses," (2) expect behavior that is consistent with their own cultural expectations, and (3) impart social and cultural skills and knowledge that are typically imparted to middle-class Euro-American children. Culture determines preferred personalities, languages and customs, knowledge, skills, and dispositions. Culture also determines preference for foods, odors, music, art, and sights. When the behavior of low-income black children is not consistent with behavior that is valued by certified and trained middle-class Euro-American child development workers (or persons who imitate such behavior), the judgment is often made that those children are deviant, defective, or deprived. Seldom is the assertion made that there may be something wrong with the child development worker or center. Centers where low-income black children are required, for example, to eat jellowed raw cabbage when they may prefer something a little more ethnic, centers in which these children are constantly exposed to nonmusic, centers in which they are constantly told that there is something "wrong" with their language, centers where "thing-problems" and competition are emphasized, and centers where the strategies that low-income black children have learned in the extended family, and are therefore available to them, are labeled unacceptable or are ignored, are examples of centers that are inappropriate for black children.

PURPOSES

The purposes of this chapter are twofold: (1) to help persons who provide child development services to low-income black children to become sensitive to some of the problems and issues that have been raised above, and (2) to provide such persons with a strategy for handling such problems and issues.

STRATEGY

The strategy which will be expanded on below is based on two rules: (1) All children are different, bring dissimilar experience to the child development center, and have differing needs. (2) To assess adequately the services offered by the child development centers that serve low-income black children, the evaluation must be from the perspective of the client (low-income black parents), and not from the perspective of the provider of the services.

This will mean that providers of child development services will need to know, at a minimum, the following descriptive information:

1. Why the low-income black children have been enrolled.
2. Whether the parents of the children in fact prefer different settings for their children.
3. If yes, why?
4. The kinds of problems the children were able to solve before being enrolled.
5. The children's eating habits before enrollment.

Other questions can be generated from material discussed in the problems and issues section of this chapter. The points is that if the center is to effect the best possible match between the nature and needs of low-income black children and the nature of the child development services provided for these children, this information will be needed.

In addition to this information, however, other evaluative information should be gathered. This information is discussed below under four categories:

1. Is your child development program reaching its objectives?
2. Is your program perceived to be legitimate?
3. Do parents of black children test your child development service?
4. Do parents of black children keep their children in your child development program over long periods of time?

Child development programs, like other human services programs, should have objectives. These objectives should be stated in measurable terms. When objectives are stated in this manner, one can determine whether or not the program is working. When this information is known, objectives and procedures can be modified intelligently. If child development services are to be consistent with the needs of low-income black children, then accurate and recent information about how well the program is working must be available routinely. This information should be actively shared with all persons associated with the program, especially parents.

You will also want to know the extent to which parents feel that the program is offering what they believe that they and their children want and need. This kind of information is vital for making decisions about modifying objectives and procedures. It also tells you how successful you have been at effecting the best match between what is wanted and needed by the client, and what the client believes that the program is providing. Sometimes this will mean that modification is indicated. At other times it will mean that the parents are not being adequately informed or that they are being misinformed. This information can be collected through many forms. Parent meetings are convenient, but these meetings also present problems. First, a special population of parents is likely to go to meetings. Second, some parents do not like to "speak up" at meetings. Third, the parents who come to meetings *and* speak up may give you only a partial view of how all of the parents perceive the child development service. Therefore you may wish to consider using other ways to gather information, such as questionnaires and telephone surveys in addition to parent meetings.

Information about low-income black parents who try or test child development services is also quite useful. For example, how often do low-income black parents bring their children only once? When they bring their children to the center for the first time, do they just leave them? Do they observe? Do they attend orientation meetings? These are all questions which to a large degree determine how your program is being accepted by low-income black parents and their children. In other words, you need to know how much your program is making low-income black parents feel that this is a good place for their children on first impression.

You also need to know whether low-income black parents are keeping their children in your program for long periods of time, and why. This is important to know because if they are, it may be a strong indication of something. If they are not, it may be a strong indication of something else. While it is conceivable that neither indication is related to your program, it is also conceivable that they *are* related and that the source of the indication can be manipulated. This is important to know if you are genuinely concerned about providing child care services that are both stable and responsive to the needs of the black community.

In short, to assess adequately the quality of the child development services you are offering to low-income black parents and their children, information from the perspective of the low-income black consumer is critical. Given such information, it then becomes possible to rate your program's responsiveness to the nature and needs of low-income black consumers. There are, of course, a number of ways in which this can be done. One way is suggested below.

RATING CHILD DEVELOPMENT SERVICES

Assuming that you systematically collect information in each of what has been referred to above as evaluative categories, you can have low-income black parents rate your program in each of the four categories according to the following schedule:

Schedule

Rating	Points
Superior	9
Excellent	8
Very good	7
Good	6
Better than average	5
Average	4
Less than average	3
Poor	2
Very poor	1
Terrible	0

Note that each rating is accompanied by a number of rating points; for example, a rating of good is worth 6 rating points. A mean rating point can be computed for each evaluative category by adding the rating points of all of the parents, dividing the sum of the rating points of all of the parents, and dividing the sum of the rating points by the number of black parents who rate the program for each evaluation category. In other words:

$$\frac{\text{The sum of the rating points}}{\substack{\text{The total number} \\ \text{of black parents} \\ \text{rating the program}}} = \text{Mean rating}$$

The computed number can then be matched with the rating scale. For example, a mean rating of 6.5 would mean that in the eyes of the low-income black parents served, your program is somewhere between very good and good. On the other hand if the mean rating is 3.5, low-income black parents on the average see your program as being somewhere between average and less than average. These ratings can be charted in the following manner:

	9	8.5	8	7.5	7	6.5	6	5.5	5	4.5	4	3.5	3	2.5	2	1.5	1	0.5	0
Objectives										X									
Legitimacy			X																
Test															X				
Holding power								X											

This fictitious program would be rated as somewhere between average and better than average when it comes to meeting its objectives, excellent with respect to providing low-income black parents with what they want and need for their children, poor with respect to receptivity, and somewhere between better than average and good when the average low-income black parents involved think about the long-term stability and responsiveness of the program. If you were interested in determining the parents' perceptions of the total program, the four mean ratings could be averaged, that is, $4.5 + 8 + 2 + 5.5 = 20$. Twenty divided by 4 equals five. In the eyes of the involved black parents, this program would then be rated as better than average.

For those who elect to use this system the following rules of thumb might be helpful:

1. If your program is rated between 7.5 and 9, you are probably doing an excellent job, and you are probably effecting a good match between the nature of the child development services and the nature and needs of low-income black children.
2. If your program is rated somewhere between 5.0 and 7, you are probably doing a fairly good job and have been able to arrive at a fairly good match.
3. If your program is rated between 2.5 and 4.5, you are running a typical center, and you ought to

improve the child development services that you are offering to low-income black parents and their children or "leave it alone."

4. If your program is rated between 0 and 2, there is almost no hope for your center. The low-income black children are probably being psychologically and sociologically damaged, and it could be construed that you are doing nothing more than taking advantage of low-income black parents and their children.

SUMMARY

In this chapter we have discussed a set of problems and issues that stem from the fact that, for a number of reasons, low-income black parents are increasingly utilizing the services provided by child development centers. These problems and issues are then brought to the attention of child care providers, and a strategy for dealing with them is explained. This discussion is followed by a system to assess the perceptions of low-income black parents about child development services.

Chapter Nine

THE CHICANO CHILD

Oscar Uribe

The idea that 3- and 4-year-old ethnically different children can benefit from having a school life is widely accepted. The current controversy involves not whether ethnically different children can benefit from early educational experiences, but to what ends this school life should be directed.

EARLY CHILDHOOD EDUCATION: THE INTERVENTION/COMPENSATORY APPROACH

In compensatory educational programs, the term *culturally deprived* has been used to describe the urban low-income ethnically different child. This term is used by most early childhood education programs and reflects an intervention philosophy. The Merrill-Palmer Quarterly (1964) published a series of papers which summarized the theoretical and research basis for the belief that preschool programs for children from low-income urban families can offset "undesirable" environmental, cultural, and social "deprivation."

Since that time, hundreds of articles and books have been written reinforcing the idea that a large number of children from impoverished urban homes are failing in school because they are growing up in "deprived" and "disadvantaged" urban environments that do not provide the stimuli needed to be successful in school. The reasoned solution to this problem is to intervene in the environment and to provide compensatory education both before the child enters school and during the early years of school.

AN ALTERNATIVE TO INTERVENTION?

More papers now being published criticize the intervention/compensatory approach to preschool education. Sroufe (1970), Baratz and Baratz (1970), Hamilton (1968), and others have criticized this position for the way in which intervention takes place, for the criteria used for judging success, and for the right to intervene. Also, research findings quoted in the literature describing the philosophy have little to do with ethnicity. The research that has focused on culture has generally fit into a framework which has assumed the genetic or cultural inferiority of children who diverge from the expected social profiles. Prominent educators still preceive the individual, rather than the learning environment or discriminatory school practices, as the basis for the problem. Problems stemming from cultural or ethnic mismatchs between the children and the school have not been considered. The intervention approach causes educators to apply simple solutions to complex problems.

Examined from an anthropological and sociological perspective (e.g., Wax, 1971; Leacock, 1969, Munuchin, 1969), diverse cultural and ethnic groups in the United States have persistently maintained their separate identities. But the schools are not designed to support the growth and development of different children. And ethnically different children are failing in schools because they have a different culture, life style, or language.

Nearly all U.S. schools are designed to serve the white middle-class child who holds white middle-class values, or the children of those adult members of an ethnically different group who want their children to emulate the white middle-class. The schools respond to these children and nurture their development. The school's responsiveness is evident in both process and content; that is, educational processes emphasize white middle-class motivational and value factors, and the educational content reflects white middle-class materials, activities, and history. In effect, the schools produce schooled citizens who are oriented to the white middle-class and who hold similar values.

EARLY CHILDHOOD EDUCATION: THE FAMILY MILIEU

I have argued that in its most general sense, preschool education in the United States serves a national ideal, which is to assimilate all cultural and ethnic differences into the American melting pot. This ideal has not been a reality, for U.S. education has been built around the white middle-class values. However, white middle-class culture, imbedded in nearly all public learning institutions, needs to be discounted when children who have been neither reared nor acculturated in a middle-class milieu are being served.

Can the U.S. public school system, whose major school programs are based on the needs of the white middle-class way of life and directed toward the objectives of acculturation and assimilation, ever hope to serve the Chicanito,[1] who is influenced by many cultures, some of which are completely ignored by the function of his school?[2] The only reasonable answer is no. Despite the many laudable attempts to improve the relevancy of preschool education of ethnically different children, many ethnically different people believe that the definitions being made and the forms chosen to implement these attempts are geared more toward keeping things the same rather than making progressive changes. Williams (1971) has stated that

> Both [minority and Anglo] have learned—the minority to his impatience and deepening frustration, and the Anglo to his pleasure and relief—that the American sociopolitical system is designed to, and does, absorb a greater number of minority groups' demands than ever believed possible—absorb them without altering the patterns, pace, or practice of society, without altering the foundations one millimeter.

In most early childhood education programs in the U.S. today, educational relevancy for ethnic minorities is nonexistent. When one considers education in terms of culture, values, and ethics (generally social education), serious differences between ethnic relevancy for ethnic minorities and ethnic majorities are immediately evident.

The push for new conceptions of relevancy is coming from concerned minority groups. Clearly there are choices to be made among quite contrary points of view as to what constitutes optimal functioning and development for ethnically different children. And minority groups are demanding the right to make those choices. It is a form of wishful thinking to believe that all preschool educational models have fundamentally the same goals and that differences concern only how best to accomplish these goals.

In preschool education, the whole learning milieu of the child must be considered. There are no neutral events in the classroom.[3] All the things that happen in the classroom—between the child and the teacher, between the child and other children, between the child and the things and experiences prepared for him—are forces of influence which inform the child of the nature of the world and of the people in it, and provide him with expectations around which he develops styles of responding.[4]

We must analyze closely the processes by which the educational milieu itself influences child development. But evaluating the effects of a milieu is far more difficult than evaluating the influence of an individual variable. Perhaps this is why this aspect of research has been neglected to date. There is more precise knowledge about individual influences than about the influences of the milieu. It would be helpful if one could understand the dynamic interaction between the child and the environment in terms and concepts similar to those used in individual influence analysis.

EDUCATIONAL FAMILY MILIEU: THE CHICANITO

The basic assumptions underlying most early childhood education programs designed for use by Chicanitos either deny certain aspects of the Chicano[5] culture or propose corrective measures that separate him from his culture.[6] The purpose of programs which hold these assumptions has been to help the establishment modify "ethnically different" behavior. To assume that the Chicano family structure is a major obstacle to social advancement, or that Chicanos create and perpetuate their own problems leads to only one solution: To remove as much as possible the conditions that "handicap" the children. Restructure the family and alter the culture and ethnicity. It is believed that this solution will "cure" the "culturally disadvantaged." This point of view fails to appreciate the Chicano family's life experiences. Such a position does not allow one to view the Chicano family as a distinct entity, and it denies the Chicano family the right to be different.

If we are to avoid destroying the Chicano family and culture, early childhood education programs must reflect ethnicity and culture,[7] as well as diversity and pluralism. And since we believe that more efficient learning occurs when the learning environment closely matches the child's knowledge and experience base, the preschool education of Chicanitos is best accomplished in a Chicano family milieu.[8]

FAMILY RESEARCH: A REVIEW OF THE LITERATURE

In all cultures considerable importance is attached by custom and by law to the family as a social unit. Each culture gives the family significant status and identity by means of support and acceptance. Therefore it is not surprising that family research is an area of concern to scholars.

Attempts to determine the level of sophistication of family theory, the types and frequency of research methods employed in family studies, and the degree of utilization of family research have been made by several research teams. These research teams have reached several conclusions:

1. There is uneven attention to the family as a whole.
2. There is frequent use of data collection techniques that involve minimal contact with the family.
3. There is an increasing use of the longitudinal study in family research.
4. There is progressively more efficient use of statistical techniques in analyzing family research results.
5. There is a general lack of hard data resulting from empirical research on the family.
6. There is a paucity of bridges between theory and action.
7. Family theory and research are relatively recent concerns, and results are poorly disseminated, making access to these results difficult.
8. Unified sets of family theory and typologies of family units have not yet been fully developed.

When it comes to actually studying families, it turns out that no one knows what to look for or what to look at.[9]

THE CHICANO FAMILY IN NORTH-AMERICAN FAMILY LITERATURE

In all societies, institutions are established to repress or oppress the needs of those individuals who oppose them. Socially sanctioned institutions are assigned the responsibility of maintaining the status quo. U.S. society, based on the white middle-class value system, has worked to remove all ethnic and cultural differences. Through its agencies, institutions, and professional planners and administrators, American society has generally misunderstood, minimized, and often participated in the destruction of many positive factors in the Chicano family framework. It has denied the Chicano family a positive status and identity, has excluded it from community activities, and has given it a feeling of alienation.[10] A number of articles have dismissed the Chicano family after presenting it in the light of the traditional patriarchal family with an authoritarian father, a submissive mother, and children somewhere between the two. Not only is this simplistic approach too gross to be valuable, but the assumption that structural patterns alone determine the value orientations of its individual members is inaccurate. The same variations that exist in any other ethnic group also exist in the Chicano family, and many factors cause these structures to vary and change.

The social science literature on the Chicano[11] family is extensive and dates back to at least the early 1900s. This literature has characterized the Chicano at extreme ends of a behavior continuum—seldom in the middle. Chicanos are characterized either as villainous, ruthless, tequila-drinking bandidos and philandering machos, or as courteous, devout, fatalistic peasants. Numerous educational, sociopo-

litical, and socioeconomic accounts by non-Chicano inves-
tigators, pursuing the quaint and curious, have added
substantially to complicate the issue further. Many studies
by so-called authorities have described the Chicano family
in such terms as "familistic," "extended," "paternalistic,"
"traditional," "authoritarian," and "marginal." Focusing
primarily on pathology rather than diversity, such studies
inevitably have blamed a Chicano family's low status in the
United States on the Chicano family itself, and have at-
tributed a Chicano family's relatively good position in the
socioeconomic system to assimilation and acculturation.

Much of what has been written about the Chicano family is value-laden, ethnically oriented, and invalid. In testimony presented at El Paso, Texas, before the Cabinet
Committee Hearings on Mexican-American Affairs, Dr.
Ralph Guzman (1967) rightly reminded researchers of
their responsibility to people in any attempt to conceptual-
ize in the area of the humanities.

> Minority research results have for centuries determined
> the concepts, images, and popular stereotypes of what
> the majority and the minority think of each other, and
> of themselves. By the theories and concepts that such
> research supports, by the results it selects to emphasize,
> and by the values it endorses, minority research holds
> up a mirror to society. The degree to which that mirror
> distorts, the society suffers. Minority research has fo-
> cused upon the individual within the system. The real
> question is not to know the minority, but to know the
> failure of societal institutions to relate effectively to
> members of minority groups. The real emphasis should
> be placed on the malfunctions in the total system, and
> not on some supposed personality traits in the individ-
> ual which endorses the fallacious notions of racial inferi-
> ority, low intellectual capacity, social maladjustments,
> cultural deprivation, social alienation, marginality, and
> lack of acculturation. Certain cultural anthropologists
> have unduly transmitted aspects of the Mexican-Ameri-

can people into presupposed patterns of behavior. A romanticized picture of reality has obscured the salient problems of the Mexican-American people. Modern day researchers have swindled the American people into believing that the quixotic and picturesque represent permanent cultural essences. A quest for the quaint and curious is not science, nor is it likely to be a service to progress. Mexican-Americans have not been well served by those who purport to interpret them to the larger society.

Although numerous studies on the Chicano family claim to be based on empirical evidence, their findings often are open to serious question. The concepts and categories used to identify types of families have been developed by theoriticians who are divorced from the population under consideration. Being bound by class and culture, they also are committed to correcting what they consider to be deficiencies in the Chicano family's life style.

THE CHICANO FAMILY MILIEU CONCEPT: STRATEGIES FOR CHANGE

Those of us who are working to develop culturally relevant educational programs that strive for cultural pluralism recognize that our greatest potential for success lies in developing a comprehensive program which incorporates the fundamental aspects of the family milieu of each of the minority groups. Until now I have been describing the nature of the problem, reviewing the literature, and advocating that the early childhood education of minority children can best be accomplished in a family milieu. Yet much needs to be done before a functioning example of a preschool operating in a family milieu can be accomplished. Tremendous amounts of research data on culture and ethnicity must be compiled, digested, and distributed. The philosophy of culturally pluralistic preschool education must be clarified and refined. Teaching personnel must be trained in the methods and techniques found to be the most effective.

What can one who is concerned with this problem as an issue do immediately to rectify the situation? I offer the following suggestions.[12]

For Teachers

1. Take ethnic study courses that have been recommended by ethnically different groups or individuals to learn more about the history, culture, and language of ethnically different people.
2. Have frequent discussions with the parents of the ethnically different children in your classroom.
3. Take in as many local cultural events as possible in your area.
4. Enlist the aid of ethnically different professional individuals or organizations.
5. Become conversant in a number of different languages.

For the Learning Environment

1. The learning environment should have some elements of an ethnic character.
2. Instruction should be conducted in the language most familiar to the ethnically different child.
3. Supplementary classroom materials should include books, materials, and activities that are relevant to the ethnically different child.
4. Cultural concepts should possess the cultural and ethnic dimension that is most familiar to the learners. Gradually the cultural concepts of other groups can be introduced. Each cultural and ethnic group should eventually be brought into the school environment.

5. Considerable time should be devoted to cultural and ethnic heritage. Cultural heritage should be treated as an integral and valuable part of the curriculum.
6. Ethnically different adults, the elderly, and youth should be involved in the school environment as resource people, teachers, supplementary teachers, teacher assistants, and special speakers or storytellers.

BIBLIOGRAPHY

Baratz, S. S., Baratz, J. C. Early childhood intervention: The social science base of institutional racism. *Harvard Educational Review,* 1970, *40,* 29–50.

Guzman, R. Testimony before the Cabinet Committee Hearing on Mexican-American Affairs. El Paso, Texas, October, 1967.

Klein, J. F., Calvert, G. P., Neal-Garland, T., Poloma, M. M. Pilgrims progress. I. Recent developments in family theory. *Journal of Marriage and the Family,* 1969, *31,* 677–687.

Merrill-Palmer Institute Quarterly, Chicago, Ill. *Preschool children,* 1964.

Montiel, M. The social science myth of the Mexican-American family. *El Grito, 4,* 1970, 56–63.

Montiel, M. The Chicano family: A review of research. *Social Work,* 1973, *18,* 22–31.

Nimnicht, G. P., Johnson, J. A., Jr. *Beyond "compensatory education": A new approach to educating children.* Washington: U.S. Government Printing Office, 1973.

Penalosa, F. Social mobility in a Mexican-American community. *Social Forces,* 1966, *44,* June.

Penalosa, F. Mexican family roles. *Journal of Marriage and the Family,* Vol. 30, No. 4, November 1968, 680–688.

Romano, O. J. The anthropology and sociology of the Mexican-American: The distortion of Mexican-American history. *El Grito,* 1968, *2,* 13–26.

Ruano, B. J., Bruce, J. D., McDermott, M. M., Pilgrims' progress. II. Recent trends and prospects in family research. *Journal of Marriage and the Family,* 1969, *31,* 688–698.

Williams, J. *The King God Didn't Save.* New York: Coward McCann Publishers, 1971.

NOTES

1. A Chicano child. *Chicanito* is used as a term of endearment.

2. Although this position is applicable to the early childhood education of any culturally and ethnically different child, I will specifically talk about this approach in terms of the Chicanito.

3. The specific effects of the milieu on the education of a child in a preschool educational setting are still unclear and unexplored. Despite the difficulties encountered in isolating and evaluating the multiple variables that operate singly or interactively to create an effect, there is a need to analyze closely the processes by which the educational milieu itself influences child development.

4. In my opinion an unfamiliar school milieu could be the cause of "cultural" deprivation. Educationally induced cultural dissonance may well hasten a child's "disadvantaged" status.

5. The term *Chicano* is used to describe those persons of Mexican heritage born in the United States. A Chicano is a Mexican-American with a non-Anglo interpretation of the world, and a non-Anglo image of himself. The term Spanish-speaking, sometimes also used to describe Chicanos, is too vague and inappropriate for use in this article.

6. Culture is a life-style determined by the collective needs of a group of commonly characterized people. Cultural life-style sets up systems of beliefs relating man to the universe. Such belief systems possess material aspects, and comprisé a group of ideas, habits, values, and attitudes. The purpose of culture is to give the group cohesion, direction, purposeful existence, and security. The totality of culture is never represented by any one single family unit. Each family unit applies what it knows of the general group culture to its own unique needs, and does so in its own idiosyncratic ways.

7. Appreciative depictions of Chicanos have not been altogether lacking. In 1940 Sanchez advocated educational programs based on the Chicano's cultural differences and geared to his customs, traditions, language, and historical background. Romano has also begun to reformulate theory that accurately depicts the Chicano.

8. Underlying our approach to preschool education in a family milieu is the important concept that the family is a system that is more dynamic and complex than the mere sum of its component parts. To be comprehensive, education in the family milieu must take into account the family system, its component parts, and its dynamic whole. A note of caution: We must be careful not to state as fundamental principles of education what is only the best working hypotheses we have been able to formulate. Only as creative educators from many disciplines and in many settings pursue the search for education in a family milieu can we create models of family milieu education that will encompass the variety of human need.

9. See Klien, J. F. et al. "Pilgrims' progress. I: Recent developments in family theory. *Journal of Marriage and the Family, 31,* 667–687, 1969; Ruano, R. J. et al. Pilgrims' progress. II. Recent trends and prospects in family research. *Journal of Marriage and the Family, 31,*

688–698, 1969; and Handel, G. *The psychosocial interior of the family: A sourcebook for the study of whole families.* Chicago: Aldine Publishing Company, 1967.

10. See Penalosa, F. Mexican family roles. *Journal of Marriage and the Family,* November, Vol. 30, No. 4. p. 680–688, 7, 1968; and Whetten, N. *Rural Mexico* Chicago: University of Chicago Press, 1948.

11. Most of the social science literature has labeled Chicanos as Mexican, Mexican-American, or Spanish-speaking.

12. I fully realize that the following suggestions, without a clear formulation of the elements to be included in an educational family milieu, are at the same time specific and vague. I am working toward developing a philosophy for an early childhood education program based on a Chicano family milieu. Until it is completely formulated, I suggest that teachers who wish to work toward constructing early childhood education programs with a family milieu rely on their own professional and personal judgments.

Chapter Ten

THE FILIPINO CHILD

Mila Pascual

The thousands of immigrants to the United States from the Philippines, most of whom came in the past decade, share many of the experiences of other immigrant groups. They left their homeland seeking a better life and greater opportunities for their families. They settled in communities of their own people, primarily in the large cities of the American West Coast. They immediately faced the challenges of adapting to strange customs in a frighteningly large and fast-paced land.

As one of our most recent immigrant groups, the Filipinos have been forced to deal with the greater impersonalization, mechanization, and alienation of modern American society, often in brutal confrontations that earlier immigrant groups were spared. Compounding the frustrations of assimilating an alien culture and society is the fact that many Filipino immigrants are educated professionals, forced into a new struggle to use their talents and training. Barriers of language and culture have relegated many people of respect and authority in their native land to often demeaning positions in this country.

Having worked hard for an education in the Philippines and respectful of professionalism, Filipino parents place great faith and hope in the education their children receive in their new homeland. Eager to take their place as contributing members of American Society, Filipinos are receptive to the efforts public schools and child care centers make on their children's behalf. The interest and enthusiasm they feel for their children's education often turns sour as they witness the insensitivity and neglect with which their rich cultural and social heritage is treated. They view the inevitable Americanization of their children not as a complement and supplement to their traditional values, but rather as a threat. Filipinos value nothing more than their children, and nothing frightens them more in this strange new land than the thought that in a few short years their children will lose the heritage and identity that has developed over countless generations.

Public schools and day care centers must recognize this source of conflict in Filipino families and must try harder to affirm the identities of the children by incorporating elements of their traditional culture in the educational program. This chapter delineates common areas of conflict with specific examples and suggests a curriculum that will attract the support of the Filipino community.

FAMILY BACKGROUND

Filipino families moving to San Francisco generally have gravitated to the noisy, crowded central part of the city known as South of Market. Low rents and proximity to jobs attract newly arrived immigrants, whose first priority is to save enough money to buy a home of their own. Just as every immigrant group before them, Filipinos gather in neighborhoods and communities of their own, where they can share with their countrymen the difficulties of adjusting to a new home, and where they speak their native language and practice their traditional customs.

Filipino home life bears directly on the attitudes and expectations their children bring to the school or children's center. At home the authority of elders is never questioned. Children look to adults to set limits and regulate behavior. Consequently, many Filipino children appear unusually shy and withdrawn in the classroom. Similarly, many day care programs that stress the children's own initiatives and informal relationships to teachers unsettle parents who themselves view teachers as authority figures commanding distance and respect.

Traditionally in Filipino families, grandparents, siblings, or relatives share the responsibility of caring for the children. In coming to the United States, many families undergo a variety of stresses that force mothers to look outside their families for child care help. The most common reason is economic necessity, which forces many mothers into the labor force. Filipino mothers often bear a burden of guilt for not being able to raise their children as they themselves had been raised, so they view child care services with apprehension. The children likewise find the situation alien, especially if the child care center environment departs radically from their home environment.

Filipino children face a bewildering array of unfamiliar experiences. Usually no one speaks or understands Tagalog, the language they speak at home. They never eat familiar foods at snack time or lunch. They never hear the fables or folk tales their parents tell them at bedtime. They never sing the songs or dance the dances they do on traditional festive occasions. The more confused small children become, the more they withdraw and the less they respond.

Filipino children are brought up in a culture in many ways more conservative than American society. Sex is never discussed with children, and parents react firmly if they find children discovering themselves. The children, in turn, react with giggles and self-consciousness to women with large breasts, revealing necklines, short skirts, and heavy makeup.

Sex roles are fairly clearly delineated. Boys are expected to be tough, active, and brave and to fight back when challenged. They never do housework, or even less, play with dolls. Girls, on the other hand, are encouraged to be domestic, gentle, and to seek the protection of the boys. Climbing trees and other "boyish" activities are rarely attempted by Filipino girls.

Filipino parents are very protective of their children. Mothers commonly breast feed their children until the ages of 3, 4, or 5 years. Similarly, many parents help their children with school projects, feeling the teacher will appreciate a well-made project more than one made only by the child. Neatness and prettiness often count more than the process involved, which, of course, is more important to the child's development.

TAGALOG

Tagalog is a very simple language. It has just one form for is, are, was, and were, which is *ay*. Consequently, many Filipinos confuse the tense and agreement of *to be* verbs in English. In addition, Tagalog has no definite pronoun to distinguish genders. Both *he* and *she* are translated *siya,* so many Filipinos confuse the use of *he* and *she* and *his* and *hers*. Another common source of confusion is the Tagalog word for yes, *o-o,* which often sounds like the English expression for no, *uh-uh.*

Both because they may be shy among adults and because they may be embarrassed about their language ability, many Filipino children will not ask questions if they don't understand what the teacher has said. If they do ask for explanations, questions will usually be directed toward a playmate rather than the teacher.

PROPOSED CURRICULUM

I suggest the following additions or modifications to pre-school programs to serve the special needs and desires of the Filipino community:

Perhaps the most basic expression of Filipino culture and tradition comes in the native language, Tagalog. Exposure to Tagalog in the child care center not only affirms the child's sense of identity, it also minimizes barriers to communication. Children should enjoy the freedom to express themselves in whatever way comes naturally. Proficiency in English will come naturally in time. The opportunity to experience the language spoken at home and English as coequal forms of communication encourage the child's sense of self-worth, rather than hindering his social development as some people callously contend.

The children should have the opportunity to read stories in Tagalog or to hear them read by the teacher. The children should learn the Filipino alphabet as well as the English alphabet.

The music and movement activities universal to preschool programs provide excellent opportunities to expose the children to traditional Filipino songs, dances, and musical instruments.

Snack and lunch times can become educational experiences if the children participate in preparing simple, traditional Filipino foods.

ACTIVITIES

The teacher can make a picture alphabet as follows:

A	aso (dog)
B	bao (coconut shell)
K	kabavo (horse)
D	damit (dress)

E   elepante (elephant)
G   gunting (scissors)
H   haligi (post)
I   ioon (bird)
L   lata (can)
M   mata (eye)
N   niyog (coconut)
NG   ngipin (teeth)
O   orosan (clock)
P   pusa (cat)
R   relo (watch)
S   sapatos (shoes)
T   tali (string)
U   ulo (head)
W   walo (eight)
Y   yelo (ice or snow)

The appendix contains a suggested reading list of modern and traditional stories and fables.

Several Filipino children's songs are available on recordings including Bahay Kubo; Leron, Leron Sinta; Ulan, Ulan; Ako ay Nagtanim; Awit ng Pagbilang; Manang Biday; Pamaskong Awit.

The numbers from one to ten are isa, dalawa, tatlo, apat, lima, anim, pito, walo, siyam, and sampu.

Traditional snacks which the children might enjoy, the ingredients for which are available at any of the many Filipino grocery stores in San Francisco, include fried camote, fried banana, matamis na kamote, matamis na saging, boiled mango, polboron, puffed pinipig, boiled peanuts, fruit salad, tsamporado, and cantaloupe mixed with sugar, water, ice, and sometimes milk.

The simplest effort can make an enormous difference in providing a comfortable, supportive environment for small children. Every child care worker charged with the responsibility of providing stimulating new challenges for little Filipino children should demonstrate a sensitivity and awareness of the special contributions the children them-selves can make to the vitality and excitement of the center.

GENERAL SUGGESTIONS

Filipino parents are interested in their children and will express this interest and participate in the activities of the center if given the opportunity. The center staff should try to visit the children's homes and should invite the parents to spend time at the center during the day when possible. Parents also appreciate tangible evidence of their chil-dren's progress, so the teacher should keep a record of each child's progress.

BIBLIOGRAPHY

Aruego, J., *Juan and the Asuangs.* New York: Charles Scrib-ner's Sons, 1970.
————. *Look What I Can Do.* New York: Charles Scribner's Sons, 1971. 1R————. *The King and His Friends.* New York: Charles Scribner's Sons, 1969.

Bartosiak, J. *Dog for Ramon.* New York: Dial Press Inc., 1966.

Cheney, C. *Peg-Legged Pirate of Sulu.* New York: Alfred A. Knopf, 1960.

Cordero, G. F., *Horgle and the King's Soup.* Manila, Philip-pines: PAMANA, Inc., 1965.

Fenner, C. *Lagalag, the Wanderer.* New York: Harcourt Brace Jovanovitch Inc., 1968.

Luna, F. T., *Pulanito (The Ant).* Manila, Philippines: PAMANA, Inc., 1962.

Robertson, D. L., *Fairy Tales From the Philippines.* New York: Dodd, Mead and Company, 1971.

Rowland, F. W. *Little sponge fisherman.* New York: G. P. Put-nam's Sons, 1969.

Sechrist, E. H. *Once in the first times.* Philadelphia: Macrae Smith Company, 1949.

Chapter Eleven

THE CHINESE CHILD

Roderick Auyang

The first indication that the American system of educating Chinese children might have been inadequate surfaced at about the same time the immigration quota was filled in the mid-sixties. Until that time, every two or three months, some police commissioner would stand in front of the Rotarians or the Lions to testify to the stability, industriousness, and general good citizenship of Chinese youths. The commissioner would even venture an assumption that a traditional Confucian upbringing, emphasizing filial piety and respect for law and order, was at the bottom of it all.

Then came the lifting of the quota and the tremendous influx of new immigrants from Hong Kong and other parts of East Asia. The impression was that every single one of them was squeezed into the San Francisco Chinatown area. The slums, long since established, now seemed about to burst. The hustle and bustle could not disguise the tension and the anxiety.

All of a sudden, or so it seemed, the behavior of Chinese children changed for the worse. The same police commissioner who had been so fulsome in his praise now found himself condemning youth gangs and making accusations of robbery, extortion, and murder. A community that prided itself on its large number of scholarships and academic awards now found among its members an equally large number of dropouts and malcontents. The resultant frustration was brought into sharp focus by a heightened sense of social awareness. The overwhelming majority of Chinese people came from places where Chinese is the predominant language, and most of them speak little if any English. A few have come to join their relatives, but most have emigrated dreaming of the economic and psychological stability that cannot be found in places like Hong Kong and Taiwan. Relieved at being able to leave the overcrowded and crime-infested slums of their homeland, they arrived here only to find that they may have jumped from the frying pan into the fire. Language and cultural barriers keep them walled in an environment worse than what they had experienced before. Some elect to go back, but most decide to stay and make the most of it. This means working long hours and saving enough money to pay for the downpayment on a house somewhere in the "avenues." This is the only way to achieve respectability and comfort.

It is obvious that Chinatown claims many families in which both the husband and the wife are breadwinners, and the need for child care services in the community is therefore acute. This fact is confirmed by the long waiting lists at each of the child care centers in the area.

These conditions also help us understand the attitude of the parents about their children. The children are, on the one hand, the end to the parents striving for material comfort. ("We do it for their security.") On the other hand, the children are the means as well. They can contribute toward achieving this security by following the well-established pattern of academic excellence and a well-paying professional career ("my son the doctor").

This attitude is of course neither new nor unique. The Chinese saying, "Establish your good reputation so that your parents may be honored," still appears in the form of newspaper columns and press releases about the new PhDs and MDs—proving once again nothing is mightier than an idea whose time is gone.

From the very beginning, Chinese children are regarded only as miniature adults whose sole function is as a receptacle for edification. Children's books are written by people who have little understanding of childhood; the consistently reiterated dictates are respect your parents and work hard. I remember going through the catalogues in libraries and being struck by the sanctity of Chinese fairy tales and folk tales intended for the entertainment of children.

Entertainment, apparently, is unsuitable for children. After all, "Industriousness pays, while fun and games bring no rewards." In this dictum, the word *pays* is indeed the correct term. Back we go to the idea of academic excellence and well-paying professional careers. So a mother who comes to pick up her child does not ask, "What did Ming do today?" but "What did Ming *learn* today?" And learning is not associated with being friendly or cooperative—nothing as vague as that. They would like the children to spell and to write, in other words, to do well in school subjects.

This is the problem: The parents hold on very tightly to their children because in this hostile and alien environment they are their most prized, if not their only, possessions. This means that the youngsters should be close to them, not only physically, but spiritually as well. They should behave in such a way that the older people can understand—keeping the customs of the old country, for example.

At the same time, they realize that for their children to do well in school in this new environment, they have to learn a new way of life—a new language, a new culture. If the children can speak only Chinese, then there is no way for them to advance academically. On the other hand, if the children adapt to the new system so well that they speak

English most of the time, that they express a preference for American food and an American way of living and thinking, the parents are likely to feel that their most prized possessions are slowly getting out of their grasp. It certainly does not help when a child comes home, speaks to them in a "foreign" language, and calls them stupid when they do not understand.

Now we begin to gauge the mixed feelings that the parents have: If a child clings to the parents, he or she may manage to preserve the old customs, but is not likely to advance and improve anything. If the child adapts readily to the new environment the parents may feel he or she is becoming Americanized and that a gap is forming between the two generations.

This is exasperating for the parents, and it does no good for the children. Either they have trouble staying in school, finding adjustments difficult if not impossible, or they find that there is a gap at home. Along the way they pick up such unfavorable nicknames as "banana"—yellow on the outside and white on the inside—and "bamboo pole"—an empty pole with both ends closed, that is, a person who fits into neither the Chinese nor the Caucasian system.

When the children are allowed to go to school with these problems on their minds, the problems may already have become very serious. And the public school system really has very little time to deal with them. It is thus left to us at the preschool level to provide a transition. Our objections may be stated very simply: (1) to prepare the children for public school; and (2) to create an atmosphere that will help them preserve their cultural heritage, so that a gap will not develop between them and their parents. Of course, both are easier said than done.

In June 1972, with a grant from HEW, a bilingual, bicultural program in the Chinatown Head Start and Child Care Centers was developed. It is a twofold program.

TEACHER TRAINING

We aim to sensitize the teachers to the special needs of our community. To achieve this end, training courses are offered to the teachers and staff members (secretaries, health assistants, and social workers). These courses deal with three areas.

Self-awareness. This course helps teachers and staff members acquire communication techniques through a better understanding of their own attitudes and those of others. Many of the problems in our centers arise from misunderstanding and misinterpretation caused by a lack of consideration toward both self and others. The hope is that, under the direction of a psychologist, the staff members can learn to be open and to listen to others.

This last objective is very important for the following reason: The Chinese have a reputation for being acquiescent (at least they did before busing). Many teachers find that parents equate criticism with rudeness and are reluctant to offer any suggestions to the staff. Another reason is that they feel they are on uncertain grounds, and that teaching should be left to the teachers anyway. However, they do not refrain from talking to the other parents with whom they are friends. It is imperative that the staff member learn to be responsive.

Cultural Awareness. Conducted by a social worker, this informational course deals with the different child-rearing practices prevalent in our community. Every day we observe the conflicts of these practices in our centers. While we do not attempt to achieve a perfect solution in our discussion, we do get closer to understanding how and why other people treat their children in certain ways.

This is important because the teachers come into contact with the parents every day, and each regards the other's handling of children with curiosity, if not distrust.

Chinese parents may feel that the teachers are too permissive, allow the children too much independence, and permit them to take too many liberties. The teachers may consider the parents too protective or too demanding. For example, a teacher might complain that a certain parent puts too many clothes on her child. Or a parent may grumble that a teacher allows her child to play with scissors, which she thinks are dangerous.

Some reconciliation of attitudes is very important. We must become aware that a child can be independent and respectful, can be creative and obedient, can be expressive and polite, and that sometimes cultural conflicts are more apparent than real.

Curriculum Development. This course is conducted by a former Head Start teacher. Under her direction, teachers survey and evaluate existing bilingual, bicultural teaching materials and techniques.

DEVELOPMENT OF MATERIALS

I have said earlier that there is a dearth of suitable materials for our centers. The second part of our program aims to develop our own materials in our curriculum development class. Doing our own research, we write our own stories. (There are already many fine stories, but few which present an environment that a child growing up in Chinatown can identify with.)

In our program, we hope to organize our activities according to the dates on a lunar calendar. Festivals and celebrations play a big part in Chinese families, even those residing in the "avenues."

1. New Year's day and the attendant celebrations.
2. Ching Ming, around Easter time, when the Chinese worship in front of ancestors' tombs.

3. Dragon Boat Festival—Ch'u Yuan. Thousands of years ago a patriotic poet committed suicide by jumping into a river after he was banished by his king. Since that time, the Chinese have been holding dragon boat races and eating glutinans rice dumplings. The festivities take place on the fifth day of the fifth moon. The races are held to scare away any sea monster which may disturb the patriot's body, and for those monsters who are particularly brave and reckless, the dumplings are tossed into the water to satiate their hunger so that the corpse will not be eaten.

4. Moon Festival. Legends are plenty here, especially those of the Moon Lady and the hare. The festival is also known as the mid-Autumn Festival, and it originated as a celebration at harvest time. It is a time for family reunions and the exchange of gifts. Most notable among the gifts is the moon cake. Legend has it that during the Mongolian rule of China 700 years ago, secret messages were concealed inside these cakes, which were then exchanged among friends and relatives. The message designated a particular time at which all the Chinese would rise and overthrow the oppressors.

5. Chung Yang. On the advice of a magician, a scholar abandoned his worldly possessions and took his family to the mountains on the ninth day of the ninth moon. When he returned he found that his cattle and his home had been destroyed. The festival is also known, quite understandably, as the festival of scaling heights.

Parents expect their children to know many of these stories and customs. Fortunately, our Chinese teachers are familiar with them and can thus act as resources.

Of course, we do not wish to give the impression that

the Chinese do nothing but celebrate. We also hope to inject into our program Chinese folklore, music, art, dances, crafts, foods, and songs, for example, the standard 24 stories of filial piety. While some are gory and others ridiculous, there are some that will fascinate the children.

The fact is that parents do pay a great deal of attention to the curriculum if they find that they can approach the teachers without any nervousness, and if they believe that they can contribute significantly by their cooperation. We are developing a bilingual handbook for the parents as well as those staff members who hold parent-teacher meetings. This is primarily a book for orientation in which we try to explain what the center is attempting and to assure the parents that we are not taking their children away from them.

Gradually, the parents are becoming more involved. They substitute at the centers when the teachers are being trained, they give cooking lessons and song and dance demonstrations, and they are becoming more active in meetings. It's been my experience that the more involved the parents are in devising and planning the activities, the more communication there will be between the home and the center. The more they understand what the centers are doing, the more cooperation they will give us.

Chapter Twelve

INVOLVING PARENTS

Daniel Safran

A FABLE

Once upon a time, long, long ago, before the institutionalization of education and child care, there was no such thing as Parent Involvement. That was because there was no such thing as Parent Uninvolvement. One day a magician arrived. He went from place to place showing the people the wonders of schools and child care centers, how they could bring children together, out of the rain, off the streets, and out from under parental feet.

The people liked the things the magician showed them. They began to build schools and to convert old houses into child care centers; they elected school boards; they hired teachers; they created indestructible playthings. Pretty soon, the schools and child care centers began to work all by themselves—as magician's devices sometimes are wont to do.

At first the people were very happy. But then a monster called Parent Uninvolvement appeared at these schools and child care centers. This monster was very evil! The more a school or child care center was able to work all by itself, the stronger was the monster's attack. The monster took over the minds of principals, directors, teachers, parents, and even children. In fact, children were its favorite target because the monster knew that, one day, they would grow up to be principals, directors, teachers, and parents. And the more children it attacked, the stronger the monster became.

Only one thing frightened the monster: It was a friendly spirit called Parent Involvement. Parent Involvement came in mysterious and not so mysterious ways. But wherever and whenever the friendly spirit came, a terrific battle would take place with the monster. Parent Uninvolvement had made slaves out of many principals, directors, teachers, and parents, and they fought to defend the monster. Parent Involvement could not enslave anyone or point to any sure and safe path. Yet somehow the friendly spirit awakened hope in the people. It sang of happier, freer children, of more competent, responsible parents. It spoke of gratified, productive teachers, of more secure and less harried administrators. But the friendly spirit cautioned one and all with its profound message: "Parent Involvement isn't easy, but it beats hell out· of the unaccountable, detached, mechanical, arrogant mess we've got now. Get it together and prepare for some hard work!"

Throughout the land, people—not too many, but enough—harkened to the challenge. And while some schools and child care centers succeed, at least for the time being, in ridding themselves of the monster, many others struggled and struggled to no avail. In the midst of their struggles they would cry out, "Argghh, you've got to be kidding! We can't do it; the monster is too strong."

At these times the friendly spirit would say, "Well, try it another way," or "There's always Plan B," or "Maybe if you gave out Green Stamps."

When parent involvement is contemplated, we tend to conceive of it in terms of getting the folks *in*—*into* the school or child care center, *in* as volunteers, *in* as staff, *in* as concerned, vital citizens. The school, the day care center, the educator, the psychologist stand at stage center and court parents in the wings. Parents are left standing on the periphery. Or, to use another metaphor, the microscope is focused not on the child's world, but on the segment illuminated by the light of clinical or academic observation. It is true that the study of early childhood development has avoided structuring its efforts in artificial *time* segments. This is not the case, however, with *space*. We have, I believe, created spatial categories for children's lives, and we act as though these categories were real and separate worlds.

It is true that some of these aspects—home, school, street, and playground—"exist" and may be *studied* as distinct entities. But do they constitute such thoroughly unconnected territories as our conceptualizations suggest? Perhaps it is difficult to think otherwise because of the public acceptance of spatial categories—or the problem may be our great distance from our own childhoods. We are *in* child development as researchers and practitioners rather than as parents or children. Perhaps that is why we conceive of parent involvement in a way which tells us that parents are *out* and that our job is to get them *in*.

The issue is not for us to determine whether a segmental or a gestalt perception is more correct, but to be conscious of the implications of accepting one or the other. Our vision may be blurred and our perspective skewed by the way in which we define the universe around us. But to the extent that we are aware of the relativity of this universe, our ability to understand it will be strengthened and our research and practice will follow suit.

Fortunately, there has been an increase in the amount of literature on parent involvement and community participation in programs for young children. Unfortunately, it is now even harder to keep up with programmatic and research activities. And to make it more difficult, students of parent involvement are found in such diverse disciplines as

adult education, political science, family medicine, environmental design, developmental psychology, educational administration, and community organization—to name a few
—and they often don't speak the same language.

Parent involvement means different things to different
people. To know what we are evaluating will require
greater clarity. For each program purporting to have a
parent involvement component these questions must be
asked and answered:

1. Why involve parents?
2. In what ways are parents being involved?
3. What are parents doing and what is being done
   to them?
4. How has parent involvement come about and
   how is it being maintained or thwarted?
5. What impact is parent involvement having, and
   on whom?

In the following pages I will attempt to examine each
question, to review some basic assumptions, and to suggest
some implications for program activities that may help clarify just what is to be evaluated.

WHY INVOLVE PARENTS?

This question is one of goals. The literature[1] suggests at
least two general bases for parent involvement:

1. The conclusions of education and socialization
   research which suggest that it is "good for children." This conclusion is confirmed by a persuasive supply of staff and parent folklore.
2. The demands for participation from parents and
   community constituencies who believe themselves to have been excluded or oppressed by the
   professional and bureaucratic establishment.

Hess[2] outlines four models which serve as bases for many educational programs for disadvantaged children. Since many of these programs have components for involving parents, it is helpful to examine each of these models, their basic assumptions, and their programmatic implications (Table 12–1). For example, a program based on the "deficit" model may hope to serve children by educating their parents in home management, personal hygiene, and family planning. A program based on the "social structural" model may hope to serve children by involving their parents in problem solving, leadership training, and social agitation. In each case there is parent involvement, but its basis and manifestations are quite different.

Irrespective of a specific program model, parents may exert their own pressure for involvement. This pressure may come in ways not anticipated by program developers or administrators. Here is an example:

> An article about school bus safety appears in a popular family magazine. Several parents get into a discussion at the laundromat. One parent tells about how her daughter got a chipped tooth. After some talk about whose fault it was, there's a consensus that something should be done. Three months later a school safety committee is meeting with the superintendent about bus safety, and a subcommittee is concerning itself with the nutritional value of certain school snacks.

Another example of "unintended" parent involvement is the case of school consolidation:

> A city school system plans to alter the pattern of schools from elementary, junior, and senior high, to lower, middle, and upper schools. In several neighborhoods, "economy" will mean losing their school site and having to send their children longer distances to other schools. Fear of losing the school site arouses parental concerns about school activities and worries older families about the potential loss of property values. Residents begin

Table 12–1. Four Program Models

Model	Assumption	Program implications	
		Child	Parent
Deficit	The low-income child has had fewer meaningful experiences than the middle-class child and is thus disadvantaged in his readiness for public school.	Remediation to help the child catch up with other children.	Parent education to fill in gaps in what the parent knows about the world.
School-as-failure	The school is unable to draw upon or deal with the child's own resources.	Teachers must be retrained to increase their sensitivity to and knowledge of the child's resources and needs; school-community relations should be improved.	Involvement to produce school reform through participation in problem solving and decision making.
Cultural difference	Although not deficient, the child differs from the middle-class child and the middle-class values of the public school.	Develop and implement a curriculum based on cultural pluralism.	Involvement of parents as representatives of the child's culture and as community resources.
Social structural	Parents behave in accordance with societal demands and expectations, and the way in which they've been treated; you cannot change the individual without changing the social structure in which he lives.	No immediate program implications; the child is the ultimate beneficiary of social changes.	Involvement and training of parents in social action to identify and overcome oppressive social conditions.

to use the school for community meetings. Interaction with the staff results in an increase in school volunteers. Since the staff wants to stay together rather than disperse all over the district, they find a common issue in talking with parents. Before long, parents are involved to a degree unique in the district, and outsiders are recognizing the vitality of the school and urging its retention as a demonstration school.

In most cases persons attached to a program may have a notion of why parents are being involved that differs from the models and concepts of educators and planners. Our knowing *why* parents are involved will require a strong respect for situational variables.[3]

IN WHAT WAYS ARE PARENTS BEING INVOLVED?

This is a question of roles. The three most common roles played by parents in early childhood programs are tutor and educator of their own child; program volunteer or paid employee; adviser and decision maker.[4] Each of these roles can be delineated further. For example, David Hoffman[5] outlines five levels of decision making: complete parent control; sharing of responsibility; serving on an advisory committee; having opportunities to observe decision making and to express concerns; being kept informed.

In many programs these three major roles may be played concurrently or on an alternating basis, and thus they may be hard to isolate for study. Even in programs where there are strict boundaries to the ways in which parents are involved, one cannot preclude the existence of numerous informal parent-child, parent-staff, parent-board interactions.

WHAT ARE PARENTS DOING AND WHAT IS BEING DONE TO THEM?

In every kind of involvement parents "get an education." It may or may not be the kind of parent education intended by the program planners. Involved parents usually find themselves learning something about self-awareness, child development, health and nutrition, curriculum development, family planning, group dynamics, instructional methodology, policy planning; program management, institutional reform, and how not to conduct a meeting.

When parents are involved as volunteers or paid employees, their activities may include just about anything program staff may do. However, a key question is, *what are parents really doing?* There is a great difference between the center in which parents and staff are consigned to a subprofessional caste system in which job security depends on capricious funding sources, and the center in which the parent's role is respected and supported by in-service training and opportunities for career development.

Contrasts are even greater among those programs that say that parents are involved in decision making. Parents who are involved "because of the guidelines" may have a wholly different feeling about their participation than parents who are welcomed as partners by a staff which believes that parent involvement is vital. Parents who serve as decision makers in one program may be passively accepting some externally imposed cluster of activities unrelated to community needs; in another program parent decision makers may be exercising functional control over all program affairs.[6]

HOW HAS PARENT INVOLVEMENT COME ABOUT, AND HOW IS IT BEING MAINTAINED OR THWARTED?

What factors, in addition to the assumptions described above, have brought about, maintained, or thwarted parent involvement? Parent involvement that is the result of legislative or administrative mandate may have a different character from involvement resulting from an energetic administrator committed to community development. Parent involvement may be influenced by factors such as whether program staff were given enough training in working with parents, or whether someone is designated as parent coordinator.

Standards for parent involvement are rare. Each program is unique in its history, in the attributes of its staff, and in innumerable other ways. Explaining why parents become involved, how they are involved, and with what impact, demands an understanding of a program's life and times. I have seen an early childhood program achieve extensive parent involvement and far surpass its envious neighbors because (or so it appeared) an education coordinator arranged things so that head teachers were competing with each other for the best attendance record at parent meetings. In another setting, at the first parent meeting of a community-oriented alternative school, I heard a teacher saying, "We want parents to become involved. This is your job; you have to do it all by yourself. I'm not going to interfere; this is your thing. *I'm* going to be too busy working with the *children!*" Future parent meetings were "strangely" lacking in attendance and the staff explained that "poor people don't really want to get involved."

As a parent, I once had a similar experience. My child brought home a 32-page proposal from a school staff with the following note attached: "Please come to an urgent meeting tonight to approve sending this proposal to Washington for our refunding." Four confused parents showed up eager to give whatever help they could in this emergency. We were told that it was really too late to change anything—the notice of the meeting was necessary to show that the program had "parent involvement."

In any number of programs, parents become involved because of the promise of jobs, or "to get away from the kids," or just "to check out what's happening." Another explanation of why parents participate in schools suggests that "the protection of youth and the maintenance of discipline require parent surveillance, even when youth are temporarily placed in the custody of other adults. Thus in our society adults must journey to school to discharge their parental obligations."[7]

The variety of circumstances resulting in what is called "parent involvement" demands a case-by-case approach to its study and evaluation.

WHAT IMPACT IS PARENT INVOLVEMENT HAVING, AND ON WHOM?

For many, this is the payoff question. And the major payoff focus has been on child achievement. There has been only moderate interest in parent involvement's impact on the family, on the educational program and staff, or on the community and its institutions.

To date, the best work in assessing the impact of parent involvement has been done by Mimi Stearns.[8] Stearns takes three parent roles—tutor, paid staff, and decision maker—and attempts to hypothesize the chains of events leading from involvement to impact. The chains are based on the suppositions and assertions found in federal guidelines, program descriptions, and various position papers advocating parent involvement and the broadening of citizen participation. A number of the links in each chain are supported by research evidence;[9] yet frequent gaps are identified where additional research is required.

Stearns introduces her "chains" with the following comments:

> Describing the chains of events helps to clarify several fundamental issues and permits examination of specific linkages between parent involvement and child performance in school. Since the evidence currently available from the literature is equivocal, knowledge about specific links in the chain will have to be developed; such knowledge is probably the only way to explain why a given program of parent involvement may be successful while another program, which at least superficially resembles the first, has very different impacts. In addition,

these descriptions permit us to look for evidence from additional sources such as the psychological literature of child development and small group theory. These chains, of course, do not take into account all the possibilities, and . . . extensive research is still needed to confirm or challenge these sets of hypotheses.[10]

The first group of chains concerns the impact of parents as tutors. Stearns proposes three channels through which this kind of involvement may have its effect:

1. Increasing the motivation of the child.
2. Increasing the child's skills.
3. Improving the parent's self-image.

Table 12–2 illustrates the hypothetical links to improved student achievement.[11]

The second group of chains suggests the set of events resulting from parent involvement as paid employees. The effects may be hypothesized in five ways:

1. Increasing the community's understanding of the school (legitimacy).
2. Adapting the school's program to the community.
3. Directly improving the parent's self-image (for example, through higher self-esteem and greater regard for children).
4. Indirectly improving the parent's self-image (for example, through achieving greater social and peer group recognition).
5. Changing the home environment.

Table 12–3 delineates the links to improved child achievement.[12] The third set of chains linking parent involvement in decision making to child achievement includes three routes:

Table 12–2. Parents as Learners and as Tutors of Their Own Children

| Chain A | Chain B | Chain C |
Child motivation	Child skill	Parent self-image
	Parent learns how to teach his own child.	
	Parent gives child individual attention and teaches him new skills.	
		Parent perceives his own new competence and communicates confidence and fate control to child.
Child sees that parent perceives his education as important.		
	Child learns skills better.	
		Child feels confident he can perform.
Child is motivated to succeed in school.		
	Child performs better on tests.	

167

Table 12–3. Parents as Paraprofessional Employees in the School Program

Parent serves as teacher aide.*

Chain A Community understanding (legitimacy)	Chain B Program adaptation	Chain C Parent self-image (direct)	Chain D Parent self-image (indirect)	Chain E Home environment change
Parent learns reasons for school decisions.	Parent teaches other school employees about target children, and serves as liaison for children between school and home environment.	Parent acquires new classroom management skills.	Parent is viewed as teacher by the community.	Parent's income rises.
Parent communicates understanding of school programs to other parent.	School program is appropriately adapted to children; parent is success model for children.	Parent perceives own influence on class and grows more confident.	Parent perceives new social status and feels increased self-esteem.	Parent moves, returns to school, takes other action to improve his self-esteem.
Parent supports school programs and guides children to perform as required.	All children do better on achievement tests.	Confidence is transmitted to parent's own child.		Home environment provided by parents changes.
		Parent's own child does better on achievement tests.		

*If parent were employed as school-home coordinator, Chain A would be elaborated.

1. Increasing the community's understanding of the school (legitimacy).
2. Adapting the school's program to the community.
3. Increasing parents' sense of control over their own lives ("parent fate control").

Table 12–4 lists these hypothetical sets of events.[13]

Stearns' models should provide researchers and practitioners with a framework from which the programming of parent involvement can be better observed and discussed. We should at least be encouraged to specify our presumptions about parent involvement and have greater facility in asking—and answering—the question, "What are we evaluating?"

Because these models allow us to engage in a more thorough conceptual analysis, I would like to suggest that there are payoffs to parent involvement other than child achievement. For the sake of discussion, and for future work, I propose that parent involvement may have the following goals:

1. Creating beautiful things for community enjoyment.
2. Building more fully integrated families which allow for individual growth and greater enjoyment of shared experiences.
3. Strengthening the capabilities of children and adults for identifying and resolving oppressive social conditions.
4. Developing greater sensitivity among persons who serve on boards of directors or as elected officials.
5. Rehumanizing persons engaged in professional or bureaucratic work.
6. Encouraging children and adults to attain new levels of consciousness.

Table 12-4. Parents as Decision Makers

Chain A *Community understanding (legitimacy)*	Chain B *Program adaptation*	Chain C *Parent fate control*
Parents learn of the problems involved in making changes, learn reasons for decisions, constraints on professionals, and so on; they become sympathetic and supportive of the program.	Parents make recommendations about how to improve school program for their children.	Parents note their effect on shaping school program; they feel some control over their own environment and communicate this attitude to their own children.
Parents communicate importance of educational programs and requirements of school to other parents and to their own children.	School program is changed according to parents' recommendation; it becomes more appropriate to the particular children served.	
	Children's level of achievement rises.	
Parents support and feel responsible for success of program which they helped to initiate.		

I believe that these goals are approachable through parent involvement in early childhood programs, and that hypothetical links may be proposed to suggest chains of events leading to their achievement. Postulating such links would be a difficult job, not so much because of scanty research and empirical data, but because of a problem we have in conceptualization. Our society is composed of large, impersonal institutions. Their power over our lives is not to be minimized by any philosophical digression on conceptual or perceptual relativity. Parent Uninvolvement is only one of the monsters threatening our well-being and early childhood programs would do well to maintain and strengthen their efforts to involve parents. Yet, I believe that these efforts must be directed toward broader goals than child achievement test scores. Parents must be involved with, rather than in early childhood programs. For it is with professionals that parents can address the crucial issues of both child development *and* community development.

NOTES

1. Hess, R. D. Parent involvement in early education. In E. H. Grotberg (Ed.), Resources for Decisions, Office of Economic Opportunity, 1971.
2. *Ibid.*, pp. 274–276.
3. See Gordon, I. Developing Parent Power. In E. H. Grotberg (Ed.), *Critical issues in research related to disadvantaged children.* Princeton: Educational Testing Service, 1969.
4. Stearns, M., *Parent involvement in compensatory education programs.* Menlo Park, CA: Stanford Research Institute, 1973.
5. Hoffman, D. B. *Parent participation in preschool day care.* Monograph No. 5. Atlanta: Southeast Educational Labs, 1971.

6. Stearns quotes a typology of parent involvement in decision making, prepared by the Recruitment Leadership and Training Institute (Philadelphia). A similar list, graded according to the extent of citizen involvement, was prepared by Sherry Arnstein: A ladder of citizen participation. *American Institute of Planners Journal*, 1969, *25*.

7. Michael, J. *Conceptions of childhood and parent participation in schools*. Paper presented to the American Sociological Association Meeting, Denver, August 1971.

8. See Stearns, *op. cit.*, particularly Chapter IV, "The Impacts of Parent Involvement: Knowledge and Speculation," pp. 29–49.

9. See Grotberg anthologies, Resources for Decisions, *op. cit.*, particularly the contributions of Robert Hess.

10. Stearns, *op. cit.*, pp. 29–30.

11. *Ibid.*, p. 31.

12. *Ibid.*, p. 34.

13. *Ibid.*, p. 37.

Chapter Thirteen

CHILD CARE SWITCHBOARD

Patricia Siegel

You've just moved to San Francisco. You're a single parent and need to work full time to support yourself and your 2-year-old daughter. Where can you find good child care for her? Should you look in the yellow pages of the phone directory under child care? Check the want ads for baby sitters? Call the Board of Education or the Department of Social Services? The list of agencies that probably wouldn't help is endless in San Francisco, and the listings in newspapers and yellow pages are no more than paid advertisements. You may get phone numbers, but you also get knots of tension and worry as you attempt to procure services vitally important to you and your child.

The Childcare Switchboard developed from the frustration of many families, particularly single mothers, looking for child care and related children's services in San Francisco. Public agencies attempt to give brief referrals to child care programs under their administration, but limitations of time and bureaucracy prevent these referrals from offering much detail or reassurance on the actual program and staff in any child care center. Referrals for more informal types of child care such as play groups and baby-sitting

173

co-ops and exchanges were nonexistant before the birth of the Childcare Switchboard. The list of private preschools is long, and many middle-class families want something better than a hunt-and-peck method of visiting and choosing the best preschool for their child.

The original and primary emphasis of the Childcare Switchboard was to assist parents in forming small child care co-operatives known as play groups. The seed funding and support for the Switchboard came from the Rosenberg Foundation, a small California foundation with special interest in early childhood education. The grant was primarily a research grant to explore the social service needs of young alternative families residing in San Francisco, with a view toward developing delivery styles and systems which would speak to their needs. The project involved the three family service agencies in San Francisco as well as a variety of consumers. One hundred families were interviewed, and a large majority of them listed child care as a primary unmet need. Consumers involved in the project urged that some of the funds be allocated to initiate innovative services otherwise lacking in the community. The Childcare Switchboard/Single Parent Resource Center received its initial four months of funding in this manner. When that funding period ended, the staff collective of five people maintained all services on a voluntary basis until new funding was secured.

Within three months we received emergency funding for a three month period, and within six months we received a one year grant of $14,000 from the San Francisco Foundation. That grant has provided salaries for five staff members, office supplies, rent, and utilities.

Everyone on our staff has participated in parent-controlled co-operative child care. We are all parents, three single, two married. We have backgrounds in social work, early childhood education, psychology, but it is our common experience as parents involved in alternative child care that brought us together at the Switchboard. We operate as a collective meeting for four hours once a week.

During this time we make all administrative decisions and assign responsibilities for administrative and day-to-day work. We have and maintain special-interest roles within the collective framework, including single parent coordinator, internal administration, community contact and outreach, coordination of special activities, and coordination of special events.

We are located in a large old house in a residential neighborhood that attracts many young families. The Switchboard itself consists of a renovated basement with two phones, one desk, comfortable chairs, couches, and a small library area. We use the garage for our mimeograph work and clothing exchange. The first floor of the house is the home of the Growing Things Playgroup, which meets daily from 10:30 to 4:00. The second floor is the residence of the single mother and child whose own frustrations and inspiration gave birth to the Switchboard. It's a comfortable sharing of space.

We are open Monday through Friday from 11:00 AM to 5:00 PM, and we've recently purchased a phone recorder which makes it possible for us to get back to working parents who aren't free to call during those hours.

The nature and scope of the services offered at the Childcare Switchboard/Single Parent Resource Center has grown considerably in our 18 months of existence. In the early months we offered information and referral on informal child care including play groups (formation and setup), baby-sitters (regular and occasional), exchanged baby-sitting, and some established public and private programs. We also offered information and referral relevant to single parent survival. This included a shared housing file and resources in areas of health, welfare, and legal aid. We received an average of eight calls a day, primarily from the "alternative" community. In addition to the services offered via the phone or visits, the Switchboard holds weekly rap groups related to parenting, child care, and single parents. We provide child care for all the rap groups, led by the Switchboard staff and occasional guests. A clothing exchange for children and pregnant women, a toy library and exchange for play groups, and a small lending library of literature in areas of child care, early childhood development, parenting, and single parents were also projects developed in the initial phase of the Switchboard.

The idea for a newsletter documenting and announcing activities, events, and issues related to children and child care came in the beginning phase of our program. It was clearly impossible, from the very start, to communicate via telephone all the little but important bits of information that make life fuller for parents and children. After 10 months of operation, we published our first issue of the now bimonthly, "Children's News from the Childcare Switchboard." Our original mailing list was 300 and our next issue will be mailed to over 1500 individuals and organizations.

We strive to make the newsletter truly informative and concrete. Its features are titled Childcare Events-Activities-Meetings, Current Rap Groups, Single Parent Page, Connecting (for play groups and co-ops who need new members), For Kids Only (children's activities and events); and a one-page make-it-yourself toy or equipment pattern. The front page is devoted to news of the current activities and perspectives at the Switchboard.

Our work in the first year quickly revealed that the most urgent need for child care information and referral comes from working parents who need full day care. Publicity of our services via mimeographed flyers, silk-screened posters, and several small mentions in the local press nearly doubled our average rate of calls within the first six months of operation.

Our logs show a steady rise in the number of calls received and areas represented by the calls since November 1973. As of March 1974 we reached the saturation point for the number of calls one staff member can handle in one day: 15. We now attempt to have two staff members in the office at all times, and our average intake is between 25 and

30 calls per day. An average information and referral call requires between 10 and 15 minutes of staff counseling. Complicated situations, special problems and emergency calls often require as much as 30 minutes of phone time.

We have grown by mandate and demand from an essentially small alternative-oriented service to an organization and service which has roots and support throughout the San Francisco community. To enlarge, improve, and update our referral network and resources we have engaged in extensive community outreach work, including contacts with public and mental health units, neighborhood organizations, community colleges, state universities, child care activist individuals and organizations, and the wide range of child care centers and preschools to which we make referrals. We make a special effort to visit and maintain steady contact with the informal programs to which we refer parents. At this point it is impossible to visit personally all the public and private programs we list, but through our work in the community and a wealth of personal contacts, we are able to maintain a sensitive perspective of the programs and staff in these centers. We have our favorites, and we do not pretend to be unbiased in our referrals. We are not there to duplicate another standard, straight referral. People who call us want something more; they want personal experience and subjective evaluation. When we make referrals we are able to talk about centers in terms of our own child care needs, and the questions, "Would we send our kids there?" And "Would we leave our kids with that sitter?" are paramount in our evaluation of child care centers.

We take the responsibility for referring families to informal child care which is not regulated or checked by any other agency very seriously. We interview all potential baby-sitters in our office. When we visit a home, alternative school, or play group we consider safety, program, styles of nuturance and parenting, and many other details. We have to assess the inadequacies of programs that have no funding or other outside support. It's not an easy task, but we go at it with a real sense of commitment and support to the parent and people who want to provide good child care to a community which is often ineligible for public programs, too poor for private ones, or looking for real education alternatives.

We know of at least 15 great centers or homes that care for from six to 20 kids all day. Few of them have adequate outdoor space; few of them would meet with either county or state licensing requirements, but they have dedicated, creative, warm, and committed staffs who utilize every inch of space and the entire city surrounding them to provide high-quality, innovative care for children. We can feel comfortable and secure with one young man who cares for seven to nine children between three and six in his warehouse project space. They take a field trip every day, always using public transportation. His children display a tremendous sense of togetherness and cooperation, as well as an alertness and enthusiasm often less apparent in children their age. In contrast, we feel hesitant to refer parents to a full-time baby-sitter who lives in a four room flat with a nice yard and a television which seems to dominate in the children's day.

We offer all play groups consultation and support. We are in the process of publishing a "Playgroup Packet" which will contain detailed descriptions of the setup and organization of various play groups. It will also include activities and resources which seem especially successful and appropriate to play groups. (For copies of the Playgroup Packet write to the Childcare Switchboard 3896 24th St. San Francisco, CA 94110.)

We visit all play groups who have contacted us, we hold a bimonthly play group rap session which offers play group parents an opportunity to share ideas and frustrations. In our visits we sometimes see things that disturb us, and we try to be frank about our observation and make suggestions for changes when needed. But we can't ensure that the changes will be made. When, on occasion, we have felt a playgroup or informal child care group is not meeting or is somehow violating our basic standards for health, safety, and well-being, we have stopped all referrals to that group and demanded time to address the entire parent group involved.

A great many of our referrals are made to licensed family day care homes via the Child·Welfare Unit of the San Francisco County Department of Social Services. Our first-hand knowledge of the tremendous need and importance of family day care in the child care pantheon prompted two of our collective members to prepare and submit a proposal to the Social Rehabilitation Services of HEW for recruitment and short-term training of family day care providers. The grant was awarded on July 1, 1974, and the Childcare Switchboard is now actively preparing and developing a recruitment and training program to begin in October of this year. We fully expect the interrelationship of the Childcare Switchboard and Family Day Care Project to be rewarding and productive.

The Childcare Switchboard has roots of community support and trust. Throughout the city, parents are anxiously trying to secure the child care assistance they so desperately need, and other than the Childcare Switchboard, they have no central agency to turn to for help. Both the Department of Social Services and the San Francisco Unified School District now refer clients to the Childcare Switchboard. The switchboard is conceived as a nonthreatening, nonbureaucratic agency which responds in a personal, informal way to the needs of parents. We believe that this style of delivery accounts for our success and reputation in the community.

Our program and services have meaning and potential for other communities, and we are interested in perfecting our model, and articulating our goals and functions as clearly as possible. The Childcare Switchboard represents far more than a professional commitment to child care services. It is a total articulation of needs we have all felt, and a provider of services we have all needed.

Chapter Fourteen

ISSUES IN DELIVERY OF SERVICES

Joan M. Bergstrom and Gwen Morgan

Important public policy issues are now being raised at the national level about how child development services might be provided in this country. Bills have been filed which spell out a delivery system relying on a system of prime sponsors and local councils. High-level officials in the Office of Education and Albert Shanker of the American Federation of Teachers are urging that support be given to a broad expansion of child development programs, but that the responsibility for their implementation should be given to the Federal Office of Education, state boards of education, and local school systems. An important piece of social service legislation, Title XX of the Social Security Amendments, offers the potential of a universally available system of child development services, but it does not spell out a delivery system at the local level. Promising as these new developments are, those involved in these three different actions appear to be working at cross purposes.

A number of groups hold a range of different philosophies on the organizational structure for child development programs and services in the United States. Complete agreement is probably impossible among the diverse groups representing education, health, welfare, labor, employers, publicly funded service providers, private service providers without public funds, parents, community development agencies, and minority interests. Yet there can be no national consensus on a coherent national policy for children and their families until these groups can identify their common ground. If we can agree on overarching concerns for the well-being of children and families, which transcend the details of a delivery system, the process of consensus building can begin.

Consensus building requires dialogue. It is not the same thing as that impossible dream, a unanimous vote. In a consensus, a group has been involved in a discussion complete enough to allow full expression of all points of view. Finally, it becomes clear what the group decision is to be, and those who have argued for another decision are willing to support the group decision because they have been heard and the process was fair.

This chapter identifies some of the issues relating to how children's programs might be delivered, and discusses some ways of dealing with them.

PREVENTIVE SERVICES

The word *preventive* is used to identify what we believe is a gap in public policy in America. The word is commonly used in two different ways. First, it means an intervention in response to an identified problem or potential problem, to prevent it from getting worse. This is generally the ways in which the medical profession and child welfare fields use the term. For example, a typical social service definition would explain prevention services for the child and family as services that circumvent the necessity of placing the child. This chapter does not intend this meaning when it uses the word prevention.

A second meaning for preventive is a future-oriented

policy which promotes and supports health in the general population. Perhaps because of these two ways of using the word, it might be better to use another term, such as *promotive* or *supportive* of health. This chapter intends the second meaning when it uses the term preventive.

Until now, social policy in America in relation to the family has tended to be geared entirely toward crisis intervention rather than to offering community support to normal families with normal children. It will take a major change, requiring the help of many groups, to support the American family in this new way.

There are several reasons why America is the only country in the world to build its programs for children with an emphasis on problems. Historically, we have a tradition of rugged individualism and a belief in independence as a virtue. For this reason, we have equated support for families with noninterference, unless there is serious trouble. We have opposed the expansion of government into new areas because of our traditional belief that the best government is the least government. Further, we are a mixed economic system, with a tradition that many services will take place in the private sector, either as private charity or on a pay-as-you-go basis.

Our tradition that the best government is the least has led to a policy of keeping as large a private sector as possible. We are very reluctant to allow government to enter a new area. To persuade legislators we must develop an economic justification for government intervention and help. Yet how do you justify a preventive service offering help to normal healthy children in normal healthy families? Until now, to strengthen our case for government intervention, we have focused on problems and pathology—areas in which it is easier to measure results. For this reason, our public policy emphasizes pathology, special needs, family problems, and child abuse, but not overall public support for healthy goals for American families.

For these reasons, when children and families are concerned, our country does not live up to its purpose of "promoting the general welfare." Instead, we promote the special welfare, of the poor, the sick, the aged, the handicapped, and myriad other categories of special need. The very word *welfare* has come to mean almost the exact opposite of its original definition.

There are three important reasons why such an attitude must be changed as it relates to services for children and families. The first is that there are families who cannot afford the needed services, and who need community support to preserve their independence and self-sufficiency, particularly those working families needing day care. Table 14–1 details the income distribution of families in the United States and in one state.

Table 14–1. Selected Statistics on the Distribution of Family Income in 1970

Total U.S. population		203.2 million			100%
Children 0–5		17.0 million			8%
5–19		58.3 million			28%

		1969 income (% families)			
Number of families	0–$3,999	$4,000–5,999	$6,000–9,999	$10,000–14,999	$15,000–24,999
U.S. 51.1 million	15.2%	10.8%	26.7%	26.6%	16.0%

It is important to bear in mind that these figures include the income of working mothers. A major problem in public policy is the failure to distinguish between two completely different kinds of two-parent families, both at the same income level. If a two-parent family has a father earning $10,000 and a mother who does not work, the family has one set of attitudes and needs. But if a two-parent family has a father earning $6500 and a mother earning $3500, their situation is entirely different. The need for day care in this second group may be more acute than in any group in our society. Yet both families are lumped together in social policy as "middle class."

A second reason for advocating a preventive approach to child development programs is the fact that a focus on pathology will create and perpetuate pathology. A treatment view of child development programs will not support the robust health which we need to promote in the American family.

Cross-cultural research by Martin Wolins[1] suggested the following common features of successful programs:

1. Successful programs assume the inevitability of a good outcome because they see themselves as working with essentially normal children in need of help and guidance and not with sick children in need of treatment.
2. They are strongly ideological, pressing in on their wards from all directions with clearly articulated and highly valued philosophical and ethical positions.
3. They assert the child's capability to make a contribution and require him to do so.
4. They provide clear examples of mature group membership.
5. They enjoy community support and esteem.
6. They provide an older child with a peer society that stands for adherence to adult values.

A third reason for a preventive approach is to offer genuine economic opportunity. If poverty is a criterion for participation in child development programs, the programs by definition will perpetuate poverty. It is easy to see that single mothers and single fathers, regardless of their income, need community support for the care of their children. Yet it is important to avoid creating an incentive to family breakdown by favoring single parents over two-parent working families struggling to avoid being engulfed by poverty. If priority could be given to families in which there is an economic need for the mother to work, the present injustices in public policy could be overcome. Family income is not a valid indicator of the need for day care, although it is a valid indicator of the ability to pay.

WHAT SERVICES WOULD BE INCLUDED IN PREVENTIVE CHILD CARE?

A national bill that is preventive in design should be broadly concerned with the education, healthy development, and well-being of infants, young children, and youth and their families. Essential components of such a broad concern would include the disciplines of education—both early education and school-age education, health, nutrition, preventive mental health, recreation, and community support for the family.

A preventive approach would not exclude the poor or children with special needs or family problems. Wherever possible, such children would benefit by being integrated into programs designed for healthy children. Specialized programs will still be needed. What is missing is an emphasis on creating the system of programs for healthy children into which other children can be integrated.

A preventive child and family service would serve children and teenagers outside mandatory school programs. It would include a variety of program forms, such as half-day nursery programs; in-home care and home-based educational programs; family day care homes and systems; full-day group care for infants, toddlers, and preschoolers; combinations of part-day group programs and home care; before and after school programs; playground programs; play groups; family resource centers, toy lending libraries, and sharing places; and weekend, evening and family emergency care.

A focal point might be the resource centers, where families and program staff come together to share information and other things. A number of such centers have begun spontaneously in the country, because of the need for "one place to go" to improve the fragmented child care nonsystem. Although it is unlikely that every neighborhood in America can have a well-funded center for such sharing, it would be extremely useful to encourage different models as shoestring operations. Such centers would be places where people could come together to exchange information and services, to socialize and to support one another. The model is one of sharing between parents and professionals, rather than a one-way helping role for the professional. Families organizing their own lives, rather than a system of problem-oriented agencies, create and participate in this kind of center.

WHAT IS THE APPROPRIATE GOVERNMENT AGENCY TO PROVIDE A PREVENTIVE PROGRAM FOR HEALTHY CHILDREN?

Government agencies are created by laws and are generally organized by functional missions such as health, social service, education, mental health, community development, labor, and transportation.

Programs for children, a client group rather than a function, cut across the interest of every functional agency. Any one of a number of agencies could expand their function to include preventive services to children, and, in fact, with greater knowledge about the importance of childhood, many agencies are increasingly seeing such programs as within their domain. A health program for the whole population includes services for the health of children and could be expanded to include child development services. A mental health program for the whole population includes concern for the mental health of children, and such a program could be expanded to encompass preventive services to avoid mental retardation and emotional problems. An educational program for the whole population, aimed at lifelong education, could be expanded to include preventive programs for children within the context of their families. A total community development program includes all services needed at the local level by a community, including services to children and their families.

With the increasing emphasis on comprehensive services over the past 10 years, many of the functional agencies have been attempting to put their comprehensive umbrella up over the other agencies, but no agency appears willing to take shelter under the comprehensive umbrella of another. If any one of the functional agencies takes total responsibility for children's services, it cuts seriously into the responsibilities mandated by statute to the other functional agencies. A health program for the whole population that excludes services for the health of large numbers of children is less than complete. A lifelong education program that excludes young children and their families is likewise incomplete. And a social service program that serves families but excludes services to their children is also incomplete. The functional agencies therefore tend to resist strenuously the efforts of other agencies to remove a major part of their function.

A strong case can be made for making preventive child development programs the exclusive mandate of either education, social service, community development, labor, or health and mental health systems, yet the needed service goes far beyond the present scope and philosophy of any of these functional government systems.

Health and mental health public agencies have expertise in serving crippled children, mentally retarded and disturbed children, and other children and families with health problems or potential health problems. While many in this system may have a preventive philosophy, the emphasis is usually problem-related, identifying a potential problem and preventing it from getting worse. To date, professional knowledge in this field is not usually concerned with early childhood education and healthy social development.

Social service agencies have been forced through public policy in this country to focus on child welfare problems and the poverty associated with welfare dependency. A social stigma has come to be associated with their services because of the problem orientation. The average working family often has negative feelings toward the welfare system.

Professionals in the agency tend to have diagnostic skills relating to family problems, but little knowledge of how children learn and grow. Moreover, there is sometimes a bias in many local and state welfare agencies against child development programs of excellence, and in favor of baby-sitting. In the social welfare field they have often make an analogy and compare institutional care of children to day care services for children. Therefore they often equate "good" services for children with family-based and in-home care. The positive benefits of quality child development programs are often not valued, and quality monitoring is not emphasized.

In favor of the social service agencies there is a growing commitment to purchase services at the community level. This policy allows the flexibility of changing services to respond to changing patterns of demand, and offers the potential for greater coordination and responsiveness to local planning. There are many excellent models of services as a result.

For example, in Greensboro, North Carolina, a United Day Care Service Agency is acting as an umbrella agency for the city's group day care center, Head Start, and a satellite family day care system. Health care is delivered from the community health center to the children in its care.

Community development agencies have had extensive experience in community organization with a philosophy that favors parental involvement. They have relationships with local governments and expertise in community planning that are often lacking in the larger and more established functional bureaucracies. They have also been associated with Head Start. These are important arguments in favor of using these agencies as a delivery system, yet these newer governmental agencies are too weak in structure for actual program delivery.

Labor agencies understand the problems of working families, and for some time they have had funds to spend for day care. At best, they are more receptive than other functional agencies to the very real women's issues in day care. Yet they have no expertise in this field and generally do not aspire to take it over.

Education agencies, the Office of Education, state boards of education, and local schools are appropriate agencies in many ways for preventive services to children and their families. Their universal accessibility is an enormous advantage, since it eliminates problem orientation and social stigma and offers the potential of universally available services to all families needing them. Educators in the field of child development express a great deal of interest in including these services in some way as a function of schools. The education system is far from monolithic, and the thrust toward young children is coming from a number of different perspectives.

There are at least three good reasons why educators are interested in child development services:

1. The potential roles of the schools for parenting education.
2. The role of the school as the accountable agency for education of young children with special needs.
3. The empty spaces available in schools and the unemployment of teachers.

While some of these reasons are persuasive, there is no reason to believe that the schools can do the whole job any more than any other functional agency is now equipped to do the whole job.

Schools in general have not warmed to functions very far removed from classroom instruction. For example, in many communities the school breakfast program was not seen as an integral school function.

However, there are many exceptions and many areas of school life in which expansion to include child development programs is entirely appropriate. Some school systems will want to extend their educational programs below kindergarten to include 3- and 4-year-olds in part-day programs, including both children with special needs and other children. Such a downward extension is very much in keeping with education's mission of lifelong education, and when the school does it well, it should certainly be welcomed.

In Brookline, Massachusetts, the Brookline Early Education Project, which is administered by the Brookline Public Schools in collaboration with the Children's Hospital Medical Center and Harvard University Graduate School of Education, is expected to have some of the following influences:

1. To influence national educational policy toward an increased concern for the earliest years of life.
2. To serve as a prototype for other communities that wish to start early childhood programs.
3. To change the distribution of resources within school systems by increasing funds for the preschool years.
4. To draw the family, schools, and medical profession into a relation of shared responsibility for the early development of the child.
5. To shift the orientation of school and community health services toward prevention rather than remediation.[2]

Bettye Caldwell of the Kramer School in Little Rock, Arkansas, is working to demonstrate that a full array of child development programs, including programs for infants and children with special needs, can be centered in an elementary school.

Both these schools are well funded and are good examples of program models, rather than service delivery models. But they offer little help in testing how schools with service rather than demonstration funds might respond to a mandate to provide child development services.

Yet many schools are having difficulty fulfilling their kindergarten mission, and will not want to extend their educational mission further, much less expand their functions to include a preventive family-centered program. The schools have much to recommend them, but they may be more appropriate for preschool cognitive programs, educational programs for special needs children, and educational programs on parenting, than for the full range of needed preventive programs described earlier. Their drawbacks are that they tend to see early education only as a downward extension of schooling, that they tend to focus on the children out of the family context, and that they tend to be less comfortable with the noneducational components of child development programs that cannot be separated from the whole.

Further, there are now very serious problems in school financing, as erosion of public support for the concept of universal education at tax expense goes hand-in-hand with major efforts to cut local taxes. Among the functional agencies now in existence, there is no agency with a child- and family-centered preventive approach. Many existing agencies see the total needs of children and their families and would like to close the gap in public policy so that American families with children would be given the needed support from their community.

SHOULD A BILL TO PROVIDE FOR SERVICES TO CHILDREN AND THEIR FAMILIES CREATE A NEW NATIONAL PROGRAM, OR SHOULD IT BUILD ON AND IMPROVE THE EXISTING NETWORK OF PUBLIC AND PRIVATE SERVICES?

We must create a system out of the present fragmentation in American services for children and their families. The question is not whether we should or should not have child development programs, because we already do have a vast number of such programs, in centers and in homes, and millions of dollars are being spent each year by parents as well as by public and private agencies. In a mixed economy, social planning must take into account what is happening both publicly and privately, and must establish some policy goals to govern the directions for the future.

The social policy questions, instead of whether we should have child care, are the following: What is our overall social policy regarding preventive children's programs? What quality will American children's programs have? How much public subsidy will be available, and for what families? How can the present fragmented network of isolated programs, both public and private, be linked into a working system?

Any new bill for expanding day care and child development programs must create a delivery system that also relates to services provided under the new Title XX of the Social Security Amendments. Although this new social service legislation cannot make any major difference as long as it is contained under a federal funding ceiling, it has potential for long-range goals. For the first time, a federal bill is worded in such a way that, if the states choose, it would be possible to create universal, single-entry social services. Public subsidy is possible for low-income families, wealthy families can pay for their own social services, and a sliding fee scale can assure that services reach those families in the middle—those ineligible for public subsidy but not able to pay the full cost of their own services. This is especially important in the case of day care.

WHO SHOULD PREVENTIVE CHILDREN'S PROGRAMS SERVE AND WHAT ARE THE ISSUES OF ELIGIBILITY?

All parents who need or want such programs for any reason should be eligible to apply. However, it is extremely unlikely that a quantum jump can be made from the present level of services to a level that meets the total need in one year. A key issue will be what to do first, since there will not be enough money to do everything at once.

One approach would be to establish certain categories of need and to meet those needs first. This appears to be the present philosophy. Priority has been established for low-income children, and a decision has been made that we must serve all low-income children before serving the children of working mothers who have incomes above the poverty level. There are at least five major drawbacks to this philosophy.

First, it segregates children by category. A very few programs in the country are struggling to serve funded children and unfunded children in the same program, but public policy creates extreme obstacles to meeting what should be a basic American goal.

Second, it prevents a program from becoming an important center for community building, since it cannot serve its natural community and the many needs that exist there, but instead must import low-income children from other communities.

Third, American programs are stigmatized in the eyes of the working families who need them.

Fourth, it is not cost-effective. Since child development programs are labor-intensive, the key to costs is in the staff-child ratio. Controlling costs without cutting quality means maximum utilization of "slots" in the program. If programs have a wide range of children in their community which can be served, and if they are given the freedom to select which high priority needs to meet immediately when a space becomes available, the program will operate at maximum efficiency.

Fifth, the final and most important argument against the categorical approach is that it is not just. It could be defended only if low-income children have a greater need for services than families struggling to sustain a living standard above the poverty level. This is true only if a compensatory philosophy is held. If the preventive approach is taken, then it is clear that the child care needs of working families are at least equal to the needs of low-income families.

Both low-income families and working families above the poverty level are keenly aware of this kind of injustice. If two families live side by side in an inner city neighborhood, they meet the following kind of irrational policy. One mother, a single parent, finds a dead-end, low-paying job, and is eligible for government help with the care of her children. The next-door-neighbor, also a single parent, finds a job which offers training, opportunity for advancement, and automatic step increases in wages. The government may help her when her child enters the program, but within a matter of months, she is ineligible for any help. A thoughtful look at the policy makes it clear that the government is now underwriting the exploitation of women by their employers. Income criteria, when income is dependent on the child care itself, place a ceiling on opportunity. If one goal of the program is economic opportunity, then low income criteria dictate in advance that the program will never achieve its goal. In economic terms, it would make more sense to encourage working mothers to earn as much as they can, and to give priority to those who can earn more because eventually they will pay more taxes.

WHAT WOULD A PREVENTIVE DELIVERY SYSTEM LOOK LIKE AT THE STATE LEVEL?

Unlike other countries, the United States currently has little commitment to preventive services for children, and no commitment to community support for families. There must be a single accountable agency that is responsible for promoting and developing preventive services for healthy children in functioning families.

We believe that this perspective can best be met at the state level. The governor of each state should assign a single state agency the responsibiltiy of promoting the development of preventive services to children and their families. This single agency for children and families must have an interdisciplinary capability, and it must be at least coequal in policy making with any other divisions of the agency designated, if that agency has other responsibilities.

The single state agency would promote and link preventive child development programs and services, which would include full-day child care programs, recreation and playground programs, parent cooperative nursery schools, preschools, playgrounds, leisure time clubs and activities for older children, and other related programs. It would, with federal help, provide funds to subsidize families who cannot pay for services they need. Responsibility for state planning, developing standards, seeing that rates are set in accordance with standards, monitoring, gathering data by areas and disseminating it to local councils, deciding on geographic distribution of local councils and geographic allocation of resources according to needs, and developing standards for staff training programs would all fall to the single state agency.

If the state creates a new system at the local level rather than relying on an existing agency, then some method of local citizens' councils could be established. The principle should be to respect existing local structures if they are designed for children and have a preventive approach, and to permit them to evolve into a model that fits that locality's needs. Human systems are open systems, continually interacting with changing conditions in their environment, continually changing themselves. We should accept this continual change itself as the model, rather than conceiving of councils as evolving toward some future ideal.

The Appalachian Regional Commission worked with 13 different states to develop a single-entry child development system at the communtiy level. It is interesting to examine the report of that experience and to note the great diversity of models that emerged in response to differing state and local conditions. A wide variety of very creative solutions developed, and this suggests that if federal controls are kept loose, community solutions may vary widely. Such variety is probably highly desirable.

For this reason, governors would probably prefer that the Secretary of HEW ask each state to designate its own appropriate agency to deliver services.

HOW WOULD RATES OF PAYMENT BE SET?

At least during the initial phase of development, subsidy for preventive child development programs and services should probably be provided on a sliding fee scale, to prevent limiting such programs to poor children or other segregated special-need groups. Reasonable fees paid by parents would be based on the ability to pay as determined by uniformly adjusted net incomes and the number of children in the family. The subsidy paid by the government should represent the difference between the parent fee and total program cost per child.

The rate of payment to each operating program should be based on the provider's total cost to guarantee services at the level of quality determined by the funding standards of that particular state. Documentation on expenditures would be required, and a maximum allowable rate based on actual costs would be determined for each function in a budget—such as care and teaching, health, transportation, and administration. Such a rate would allow for the wide variability of day care costs.

HOW WOULD THE PROGRAMS BE FUNDED?

Some have suggested that preventive child development programs should be modeled on the public school, that is, that they should be universally available and free. We believe that the funding model for higher education is currently more useful and more appropriate conceptually. The model of higher education is highly diverse and unstandardized; there are some public education agencies, some private agencies, some public subsidies for specific purposes to both public and private agencies, and funds for scholarship available to individuals. Much private giving goes to higher education. College education is voluntary, not required, just as preventive programs for children would be at the other end of the scale, where education is not required. Programs will probably continue to mobilize a mix of public subsidy, parent fees, and other public and private funds.

A model of an uncategorical, unsegregated day care and child development program could be presented by the following over-simplified representation.[1]

If the vertical axis represents a scale from 0 to the full cost of child care, and if the horizontal axis represents a scale of poor families to wealthy families, the present policy would show that a segment of the poor population is now benefiting from quality child development programs with public subsidy under Head Start, Title 1 of the Elementary and Secondary Education Act, Title 4-A of the Social Security Amendments, and various other scattered sources. Some of the wealthy are paying for their own services. The large group in the middle—working families, many of whom need support—receive no subsidy and cannot pay the full cost of programs of adequate quality. This group could pay a fee based on a sliding fee scale. The missing piece in public policy is the other triangle, the part of the cost not covered by the fee which must somehow be subsidized to bring services within the reach of these families.

Full cost
of program

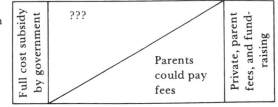

$00

The assumption of this chart is that the basic care costs of a child development or day care program are the same for any child at any income level. Children of the poor are not a different species from other children. All children have common basic needs which must be met. If a child has special needs, either physical, emotional, or intellectual, then special, additional help must be built into the program to meet that individual need. These special needs are an addition to, not a substitute for, the needs which all children share.

A major issue to be resolved in this country is the desirable relative percentage of funding from the federal, state, county, and municipal governments. There are four arguments in favor of heavy federal funding;

1. Programs could get started rapidly, without waiting to solve local or state funding problems and priorities.
2. The fairest tax base is at the federal level, since corporations cannot flee the federal tax as they flee state and local taxes.
3. Programs for young children have far-reaching effects not confined to localities or even to states.
4. Without heavy federal funding, programs will have an uneven and slow beginning, primarily in wealthy communities or in those where high community and development funds are already available.

The arguments in favor of larger state or local shares are:

1. Congress may be unwilling to commit so high a percentage of the federal tax dollar to the child development programs and services, and this factor may defeat bills.
2. Without much local share, there is not likely to be

a strong local commitment to the quality and long-range continuation of the programs.

3. State or local funding has a potential for more interagency links by encouraging public and private matching funds.

Different mixes of funding might be considered. One model might be 50% federal, and a 25% state matching share for a 25% local share. Another approach would be to start at a 75% or 80% federal share, and to reduce it in successive years to 60% or 50%.

CONCLUSION

As we all know, children are an important resource to our society. Children and their families need support and we must meet the challenge of delivering quality services which are preventive, innovative, and self-renewing.

REFERENCES

1. Wollins, M. Child care in cross-cultural perspectives. Final report. Mimeograph. Berkeley: University of California, 1969.

2. Pierson, D. E. The Brookline early education project: Model for a new education priority. *Childhood Education*, 1974, Vol. 50 No. 3 p. 132–135.

NOTE

1. This frequently used model was first developed in a conference workshop at the first Urban Research Corporation Conference on Industry and Day Care, Chicago, Illinois, 1970.

BIBLIOGRAPHY

Auerbach, S. "Child Care in the Public Schools: An Interview with Albert Shanker," *Day Care and Early Education Magazine,* Sept/Oct 1975, *3,* pp. 18–19, 53–55.

Bergstrom, J., Gold, J. *Sweden's day nurseries: Focus on programs for infants and toddlers.* Washington, D.C.: Day Care and Child Development Council, Inc., 1974.

Bourne, G., Medrich, E. A., Steadwell, L. & Barr, D. *Day care nightmare—A child-centered view of child care.* University of California, Berkeley: Institute of Urban and Regional Development. Prepared for the Field Foundation "Children's Advocacy Project." Working Paper No. 145, February 1971.

Class, N. E. *Growing up in the 70's. A policy statement for a system of state and county departments of children and parents' service.* Sacramento, California: Legislative Assembly Office of Research AOR No. 19, August 1975.

Finberg, B., Caldwell, B., Gallagher, J., & Pierson, D. *Organizing to deliver services: The public school system.* Denver, Colorado: Education Commission of the States, Report No. 58, Early Childhood Report No. 10, December 1974.

Martin, W. *Public Policy and Early Childhood Education: A Buddhist Garden.* Denver, Colorado: Education Commission of the States, Report No. 58, Early Childhood Report No. 10, December 1974.

Morgan, G. Guaranteeing quality in child care. Presented to the Regional Conference on State Services in Child Development, Education Commission of the States. Philadelphia, Pennsylvania, April 3, 1975.

Neal, T. Organizing the states for children's services. *Compact,* July–August, 1973, Vol. 4, pp. 22–24.

Pizzo, P. Public schools and day care: An interview with Albert Shanker. *Voice for Children, 8,* 1975.

A report of the education commission of the states. *Early childhood programs in the states: Report of a December 1972 conference.* Denver, Colorado: Education Commissions of the States, Report No. 34, Early Childhood Report No. 5, March 1973.

A report of the education commission of the states. *Implementing child development programs.* Denver, Colorado: Education Commission of the States, Report No. 58, Early Childhood Report No. 10, December 1974.

Young, D. *Public policy for the day care of young children.* Lexington, Massachusetts: D. C. Heath, Lexington Books, 1973.

Chapter Fifteen

CHILD CARE: WHERE DO WE GO FROM HERE?

Stevanne Auerbach

Back in 1970, the four thousand delegates to the White House Conference on Children voted to promote expanded, comprehensive, quality child care service as the number one priority. Now, years later, we see that the emphasis placed on the importance of publicly supported child care as a service to all families has largely continued. Many excellent programs throughout the country continue to struggle merely to maintain their existence, and new programs lag far behind the most pressing needs. The increase of funds and resources necessary to improve and expand services has virtually come to a standstill. Policies at the federal and state levels have been confusing and inconsistent.

The massive legislation program to provide the much-needed services should have been approved and passed long ago. But two major setbacks—President Nixon's veto of the Comprehensive Child Care Act in 1971 and President Ford's veto of the Child and Family Services Act in

Reprinted from *Day Care and Early Education,* Fall, 1977, pp. 28–30 by permission.

1976—demonstrated that this country's leaders lack the commitment to care for the young and to provide support for parents.

The White House Conference on Children lies ahead. In view of the seven years which have witnessed the stalling of new child care legislation, action before another such conference is needed more than ever. Perhaps supporters of child care services can take heart from the fact that Walter F. Mondale, co-sponsor of the ill-fated Child and Family Services Act, is now Vice President. Previously, he did not have the sympathetic ear of a president concerned and committed to the improvement of conditions for the child and the family, although his continuing diligence kept attention on the problem. Only time will tell what action is taken by future administrations.

In any event, we cannot relax our efforts to keep good existing services alive, to provide new ones, and to inform parents of what is available and what their choices are. We cannot afford to wait, because with every passing year hundreds of thousands of young children are missing out on what might be the single most significant boost of their lives toward attaining their fullest potential.

To proceed in a purposeful direction, we must have an image of what would be most desirable—a vision of the best possible future for child care services in America. We need to decide what kind of child care we want in this country, for whom it should be available, and how we are going to move toward the realization of this vision. This chapter provides one view—based on years of study and investigation, of what a positive future for child care services might look like.

BENEFITS TO THE FAMILY

A comprehensive approach to a child care system would provide for children of a range of ages, from infant up school age. All families who need the services, whether they are on welfare, working, attending school, volunteering, or using their time in other ways, could be eligible. They would pay based on a sliding scale of fees—which might range from free, $25 or $50 a week. The parents would participate in the program (beyond paying fees) in meaningful ways—and they would find their work or study less guilt-ridden and more productive.

The child care system would be responsive to the needs of the individual community. Flexible schedules, both full day and part day, with educational experiences, opportunities for creativity and multicultural learning experiences would be available. Qualified staff members of both sexes, well trained and tuned in to the language of the families being served, would have the necessary skills to meet the needs of the children. Materials appropriate to the growing and developing young child would be on hand. Indoor and outdoor play spaces with interesting and imaginative equipment would be built, and there would be quiet areas as well. Parents would be encouraged to participate through evening meetings planned for right after work, with supper and care for their children provided simultaneously. We would also see handicapped children cared for in centers and homes by staff specifically trained to work with these children so that everyone could come to understand their real potential.

A good child care facility would have a well-conceived curriculum, staff, and child growth and development oriented philosophy. There would be a feeling of home quality throughout the whole program, from the design and environment of the facility (inside and out) to the way the food is prepared and served (regular meals, snacks, opportunities for the children to shop and cook), and including the ways and extent to which parents are involved. These same principles apply to a family group care home which includes a smaller number of children.

It is important that child care facilities be of the highest possible quality. We do not want children to be cared for at any time in dismal surroundings, without adequate meals, rest, stimulating toys, health care, or someone to talk to in their native tongue. We do not want to see parents have to make do with little peace of mind and a haphazard system of baby-sitters and other occasional companions.

Since the early years are the most crucial ones in the young person's life, we must establish and perpetuate a quality-control system. To do this we must reexamine, redefine, and clarify the standards and licensing to which child care programs must conform. The standards set for child care must ensure safety, must be reasonable, and be enforceable. We might institute licensing and quality control through a public ombudsman in every community. We could prepare trained and well-respected individuals to inspect child care centers and homes as quality-control experts, much as the Environmental Protection Agency does for air and water.

NETWORKS

With the continuing involvement of parents in the planning and operation of child care facilities, active and concerned parent groups would emerge. Their functions should be to assist each other and the staff with the program and to share with each other and available specialists the nature of the role and stresses of parenthood. Networks of smaller family day care homes connected with larger centers could provide comfortable alternatives and consistency to families seeking a form of care that is compatible with their children's daily needs.

Perhaps we would also see an integration and interconnection of the professional groups so essential for greater progress in the area of children's services. Optimally, improved communication would take place among educators, psychologists, social workers, medical personnel, and others—professionals who can put aside their separate self-interests and look toward ways to enhance cooperative efforts in support of children and families.

Eventually we might see networks established among centers and homes in order to bring many additional advantages. One of these advantages would be to provide services to sick or handicapped children; another would be to encourage age mixes, as between older people and young children, to create the maximum opportunity for mutual understanding and experiencing so important to both. We must examine ways to permit children of different ages from the same family to attend the same center or care home. We must also seek ways to link up—in addition to homes and centers—schools and playgrounds, community centers, libraries, and community resources. Perhaps minibuses for children could run continuously all day, taking children from school directly to recreation centers and to other places of interest around their community. Adults would be located in each of these places to supervise and provide any needed information or resources.

We must develop a consortium of professional staff people who can work together to create an Office of Children's Services in every city and in every county. Such a bureau would coordinate child care efforts and work to find new ways for parents and professionals to communicate with each other and mutually support their common endeavors. If we provided more part-time employment or shared jobs for teachers, these professionals could spend more time with children and with other professionals interested in child care.

There is a natural link between schools and child care services. Every high school should have an infant and preschool program so that high school students can have the opportunity to learn about young children. (Some high schools already are doing this.) Such a program could also provide for young women who do not want to interrupt their educational progress if they became pregnant before graduating. More space for day care programs in public schools will become available as the school-age population declines.

I foresee part-day programs such as Head Start and other public or private nursery programs as an integral part of the child care network. A large center, for example, could offer a specific educational program for three hours a day, after which the children would go to a nearby family day care home for the balance of the day for additional play, supervision, and rest. With such an arrangement, everyone benefits. The child receives educational, social, and physical care opportunities; the parents can attend school or work; the teachers can plan for the best use of their time; and the family day care provider is brought into the system through training and other support services.

Although at this time we still lack an adequate national system of developmental child care services, many local efforts have been enormously successful. Children and families have benefited from the many programs developed and sponsored by church groups, parent cooperatives, community organizations, and small nonprofit centers. The ultimate challenge is to sustain the progress made by these efforts, the insights and experience gained, and to build upon the models and resolve the unmet needs. To do this we must establish communication links between different types of facilities.

We must also provide greater opportunities for parents to talk informally, share their experiences, and gain needed information. A switchboard service is an enormous benefit to those new to an area, or to those who need assistance in an emergency or when centers might be closed. Another such service such as a switchboard can provide an immediate response when there is parental tension or stress, and it can assist with referrals to other kinds of special services for children. Switchboards can also help to locate staff and volunteers.

ATTITUDES TOWARD CHILD CARE

The blueprints for sound comprehensive child care systems have been available for some time and with leadership, support, and determination they may become a reality in the near future. How much they are implemented will depend largely on the prevailing attitudes across the nation —attitudes that can be shaped with increased dissemination of accurate information about child care.

First, child care must be reassessed and seen as an important and unique educational opportunity. Instead of being considered only as a preparation for school, it should be seen as an ongoing intellectual and social opportunity in itself. Preschool children are ready to learn, and good child care *combined* with school can vastly enrich the total educational experience.

Second, child care must be viewed as a supportive and complementary service to the family. Parents greatly benefit from and often need a respite from their children. They can gain new insights and understandings about them from other adults and from observing other children in child care. Freed from the confining demands of uninterrupted child rearing, parents can provide for their family needs more adequately in the long run. They will be less likely to depend on welfare if they are assisted and not penalized for their efforts. They are more likely to serve as positive role models if they have constructive channels for supporting their children. Rather than separating parents from their children, good child care systems—the kind that encourage and depend on parent participation—will give parents an opportunity to take an active role in shaping their children's development

At the 1970 White House Conference the point was made in the following words:

> Because the primary need for child care is to help functioning families lead more satisfying lives, and not to

replace families, services which are not responsive to the variety of family needs will not be adequate. We must understand the process by which families choose a particular child care arrangement. In general, they are looking for supplementary care that is flexible in hours, reasonable in cost, convenient in location, and often last, dependable in quality. The challenge we face is to develop a system of services with at least three effects: making parents more aware of quality in child care programs; assisting parents in maintaining their parental responsibilities; and delivering good care to all children, regardless of the specific arrangement.[1]

Third, child care must be viewed as a natural extension of the home, offering flexibility and a wide variety of choices for the child. Children who are provided with real choices can progress happily during the day from active to passive activities and from indoor to outdoor ones. They might learn to cook, to help clean up, to listen to music, and to interact comfortably with other children.

We must strike a better balance between informal and formal instruction and between structured and alternative lifestyles, and we must see the relative values within each. We also need to develop more bilingual and multilingual programs. English-speaking children could learn languages of other children at an early age—when it is a simpler task than at later ages—and children who speak foreign languages could have greater opportunities to learn English and maintain their own languages and cultures.

Finally, child care must be understood to be a cost-effective program: although it does cost money, the returns are more than equal to the expenditure. The income earned by a parent who is free to work helps the economy. The child gains important experiences essential for growth and independence and is not so likely to be a social problem as is a neglected child. Funds spent on quality child care services are, by any standards, an excellent investment.

Raising the funds, of course, is an ongoing problem. Perhaps new legislation will provide some consistent support for child care. A successful funding formula might be a ratio of 75% federal, 15–20% state, and 5–10% local. Tax incentives or matching grants are also needed to encourage local businesses to provide various forms of direct and indirect financial support for child care in their communities. But we cannot simply wait for new legislation to happen: we will have to do some educating and spend time on innovative public-relations to bring the problem to the forefront of public consciousness.

Today more than ever, child care is needed by working families. The lack of broad support for day care programs and the continuation of the welfare stigma for eligibility clearly hinder the availability of expanded and improved child care. As a result, many children who would otherwise benefit from a healthy, exciting, and supportive environment are hidden away in empty houses and apartments. Child care added to services now available could make a real difference to the families who need or want to work.

We should be ready to make a genuine and humanistic contribution to the world of infants and children in America. All of us together must seriously consider where we are, where we want to be, and what kind of world we want for the future. Legislation and new monies alone, while urgently needed, will not provide sound policy and programs. That is up to us—parents, professionals, and others interested in the well-being of tomorrow's adults.

We hope the information and ideas presented in these volumes will be constructive to you wherever you are in your program's development. With your commitment to action on behalf of children we are certain that the children where you live will benefit from the quality child care services you are working hard to provide. We wish you every success in your endeavors and anticipate good results in the years ahead. For the children everywhere, may the adults around you always be able to see and respond in nurturing, supporting ways so the care you receive now will provide positive and solid grounding as the basis for your growth toward tomorrow.

REFERENCE

1. "Report of Forum 17, 1970 White House Conference on Children," in *Rationale for Child Care Services: Programs vs. Politics,* Volume 1, Child Care: A Comprehensive Guide (New York: Human Sciences Press, 1975), p. 161.

SUPPLEMENTAL MATERIAL FOR CHAPTER 1
SCHOOL-AGE CHILD CARE

Docia Zavitkovsky and Ida Bucher

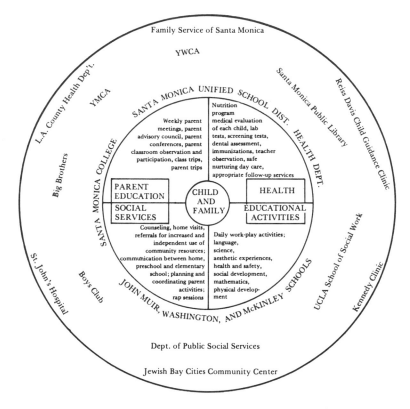

Figure A-1. Sample Administrative Organization (Part 1)

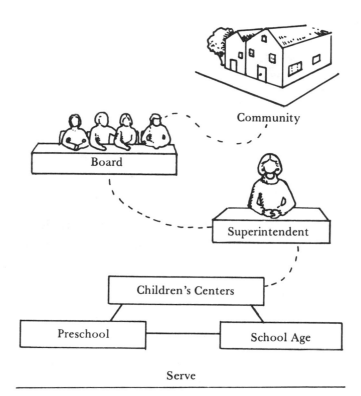

Community

Board

Superintendent

Children's Centers

Preschool

School Age

Serve

Familics   Junior High Schools

The Community   Colleges

Elementary Schools

Figure A-2. Sample Administrative Organization (Part 2)

Purpose:

The purpose of children's centers is to provide a program that meets the fundamental growth and development needs of children who are out of the home for a large part of each day. The primary focus is on the individual child and his family.

Authorized:

By State Legislation, administered by the School District, and supervised by the State Department of Education, Bureau of Compensatory Education.

Financed:

By State and Federal Funds, parents' fees and a District Tax. Fees are determined by a formula based on income, number of children, number of parents in the family and the number of hours the children are in the center.

Operated:

Under the same organizational system as other branches of the school district program. Administrative procedures related to curriculum, finance, personnel, legal requirements, attendance accounting, and the health program are coordinated with those of all other divisions of the Santa Monica Unified School District.

Figure A–3. Sample Administrative Organization (Part 3)

SAMPLE ACTIVITIES

EXTENDED DAY CARE FOR CHILDREN 5 TO 12 YEARS OF AGE (PART 1)

7:00   Center opens.

7:00 to 9:30 Arrival of children in accordance with parents' work schedules and the grade school hours.

Morning program adapted to interests, age levels, and hours of attendance in regular school classes.

Indoor Activities: Construction activities with blocks and accessory materials; music; language and literature with books, stories, discussion, conversation; manipulative materials (puzzles, scissors, pegboards, etc.); card games; study area for children who want to finish their homework; records for listening; cooking experiences.

NOON   Lunch in the school cafeteria.

12:45 to 4:30 *Afternoon Program:*

12:45 to 3:00 Kindergarten: Opportunities to help meet physical needs, and to establish routine habits and positive health attitudes. Rest, washing, snack, indoor activities.

2 o'clockers Grades 1 and 2: Children who return to the center at 2:00 PM. Snack. Indoor activities.

3 o'clockers Grades 3 to 5: Children who return to the center at 3:00 PM. Snack.

Indoor Activities: Blocks and accessory materials; puppets; dramatic and housekeeping play; puzzles and card games; music and art materials; reading corner; sewing; craft projects and hobbies; study area; creative dramatics; science and nature; cooking.

Outdoor Activities: Physical activities which involve running, hopping, skipping, jumping, balancing, climbing, such as jump rope, roller skates, kickball, punching bags, circle games, hopscotch, wagons, trikes, and cargo net; team sports and organized games; dramatic play with boxes, ladders, boards, tarps, barrels, blocks and other accessory materials (hats, ticket punches, pulleys, steering wheels, pilot's wheel, etc.); gardening; woodworking; craft projects and hobbies; science and nature projects; sand, mud, and water play (weather permitting).

215

4:30 to 6:00   Inside and outside cleanup.
                Preparation for going home.
                Individual and small group indoor activities.

6:00 PM   Center closes.

                Note: Children are released to attend Cub Scouts, Boy
                Scouts, Girl Scouts, Camp Fire Girls, YMCA, YWCA,
                Boys' Club, the public library, park activities, and to
                visit friends, but written permission from parents is re-
                quired.

SAMPLE ACTIVITIES (VACATIONS AND HOLIDAYS)
EXTENDED DAY CARE FOR CHILDREN 5 TO 12 YEARS OF AGE (PART 2)

7:00   Center opens.

7:00 to 9:30   Arrival of children. Health check. Morning program
                adapted to interests, age levels, and hours of atten-
                dance. Indoor activities with blocks and accessory ma-
                terials; manipulative materials (puzzles, scissors, peg
                boards, etc.); card games; records for listening; sewing;
                library corner.

9:30   Snack time. Children assist with preparation of snack,
                serving, and cleanup.

10:00 to 11:30 *Indoor and outdoor activities—group and individual:*
                Puppetry, woodwork, dramatic and housekeeping play,
                music and body movement, handcraft activities, cook-
                ing, gardening, walks, trips, beach, swimming at Y or
                school pools, outdoor games, camping, play on outdoor
                climbing equipment, creative writing, drama.

11:30 to 12:30 Routine activities. Washing up for lunch.
                Lunch. Assist with preparation, setting tables, serving,
                cleanup.

12:30 to 2:00   Rest time according to age and needs of the children.
                Quiet activities—books, records, card games, puzzles,
                dominoes, checkers, etc.

2:00 to 4:00   Afternoon snack.
                Varied indoor and outdoor activities, see morning ac-
                tivities.

4:30 to 5:30	Inside and outside cleanup. Preparation for going home. Individual and small group indoor activities.
5:30	Center closes.

Note: Children are released for Cub Scouts, Boy Scouts, Camp Fire Girls, Girl Scouts, and similar activities, but written permission from the parent is required before children are released.

SUPPLEMENTARY MATERIAL FOR CHAPTER 3
TRAINING CHILD CARE PERSONNEL

Lucille Gold

SAMPLE CHECK LIST: WHO ARE YOU?

1. My clearest memory of an experience with my family before I was six years old is _____
2. I learned the meaning of "being good" and "being bad" by _____
3. My (sisters)/(brothers) were (important)/(unimportant) people in my early years because _____
4. The things I learned from my family were _____
5. My family provided me with an image of the world that was _____
6. The way I felt about school was _____
7. The strongest influence during my growing years was _____
8. I believe that children need freedom because _____
9. I believe that children need controls because _____
10. A spoiled child develops when _____
11. My definition of a good life is _____
12. Parents' responsibility to their children includes _____

13. Children's responsibility to their parents includes _____
14. A child feels good when _____
15. The things I like about myself are _____
16. The things I don't like about myself are _____
17. I am happiest when _____
18. I am unhappy when _____
19. A positive social pressure is _____
20. A negative social pressure is _____

Behavior of Children Under One Year

(Remember that every child develops according to his or her own rate of growth and in his or her individual way.)

	Four weeks or less	Three months	Six months	Nine months
Motor behavior	Regards objects in line of vision only. Follows objects to midline, not beyond. Toys placed in hands with difficulty, infant drops them immediately. Attends noises momentarily with diminished activity.	Regards objects more than momentarily. May follow objects for 180°. Holds objects actively, glances at them.	Immediate approach and grasp of objects. Holds with both hands. Palmar grasp of objects. Turns head in direction of loud noises.	Radial digital grasp on objects. Prehands objects between thumb and index finger. Able to transfer objects from hand to hand.
Language behavior	Small throaty noises. Soft subvocal sounds.	Coos, chuckles. Vocalizes in some manner or "talks back" in response to social stimulation.	Vocalizes. "Talks" to toys. Grunts, growls.	Imitates sounds such as a cough, clicking of tongue. Says "dada" (Says "mama" at 10 months). Understands name, "no-no."
Social behavior	Regards faces, diminished activity. (Follows moving figures at 2 months.)	Vocal, social response (spontaneous social smile at 4 months). Great demand for social attention. Marked interest in father.	Discriminates strangers. May be shy of strangers. Initiates social play by smiling and vocalizing.	Shy with strangers, may be afraid of a strange voice. (Pat-a-cakes, waves bye-bye at 10 months.)

Developmental				
Feeding	2 night feedings after 7 PM, 5–6 feedings in 24 hours. (7–8 at birth.)	3–5 feedings per day. May indicate desire to be fed by fussing instead of crying. May enjoy being fed from spoon and cup, although much spilling will occur.	3–4 feedings per day. Eats solids well at 7 months. May prefer the bottle and solid foods to breast feeding. Enjoys spoon feeding and is more adept with cup.	3 meals a day, fruit juice in afternoon, 2–3 bottles a day. Holds bottle. Feeds self cracker. May be fed from a spoon in a high chair. Juice taken well from cup.
Sleep	Sleeps most of day and night, 20 of 24 hours, usually in 4–5 periods (7–8 at birth).	May sleep for 12 hours at night. Naps 3–4 times during day.	Usually 11–13 hours at night. 2–3 naps a day.	Usually 2 naps during day.
Bathing and dressing	Baby enjoys bath but does not like to be dressed and undressed.	Kicks and laughs during bathing.	Enjoys being undressed for bath and enjoys bath—splashes vigorously. Is able to remove booties.	
Weight gain	Average at birth is 7 lbs.	Usually gains 2 lbs. per month in the first three months.	Usually gains 1 lb. per month from 6–9 months.	Usually gains about 2/3 lb. per month from 9–12 months.
Teeth	The first teeth begin to cut from about the sixth to eighth month. By 2½ years, all the baby teeth have usually come through.			

(continued)

Behavior of Children Under One Year (continued)

Toys for first year		Clothing for first six months minimum essentials for layette
Toys to bite, shake, hold, drop, look at or listen to. Washable, large enough so that they can't be swallowed; painted with nonpoisonous paint. Oilcloth or soft animals; colored wood or plastic beads; rattles; transparent, rubber, or sponge balls; teething rings, hanging objects to look at (Cradle Gym), clothes pins, spools on string, blocks, cup and spoon, pie pan, box with cover.	Diapers 3–4 dz.	*Diapers*—cotton bird's-eye cloth, bird's-eye gauze or square-woven gauze.
	Shirts (long, short, or sleeveless depending on climate) 3–4	*Shirts*—cotton, preferably without buttons or tapes. Flat, well-finished seams, large head and armholes.
	Nightgowns or wrappers 4–6	*Nightgowns and wrappers*—cotton, flannel, lawn, batiste, seersucker, stockinette, flannelette, flat, well-finished seams, back opening.
	Sweaters or sacques 2	*Bibs*—absorbent material such as cotton outing flannel, gauze, cheesecloth, turkish toweling.
	Flannel squares or baby blankets 2–3	
	Warm hood (if cold climate) 1	
	Dresses, additional sweaters, bunting, etc., depending on climate and desires of individual mother.	
	Abdominal bands are usually provided by hospital. 3 are needed, of gauze or soft flannel, 4–5″ wide, 18–20″ long.	

Typical Behavior of Children Between One and Two Years

(Remember that every child develops according to his or her own rate of growth and in his or her individual way.)

	One year	Fifteen months	Eighteen months
Motor behavior	Can change from supine to sitting position by himself. Pivots in sitting position. Creeps. Is able to pull self to standing position. Cruises, holding to a rail. Walks with one or two hands held. Enjoys gross motor activities—putting objects in and out of other objects, etc. Pincer grasp of small objects (between thumb and tip of index finger).	Has discarded creeping unless fatigued. Creeps up stairs. Walks alone a few steps, starts and stops without help or support. Falls by collapsing (sitting down suddenly). Holds crayon in fist. Imitates scribble.	Seats self in small chair. Walks up stairs, one hand held, marking time. Walks fast and well, seldom falls. Runs stiffly. Imitates strokes with crayon.
Language behavior	Knows two words. Understands meaning of "give," and will "give" a toy on request.	Jargon. Four to six words. Indicates wants, points, and vocalizes.	Knows ten words.

(continued)

Typical Behavior of Children Between One and Two Years (continued)

	One year	Fifteen months	Eighteen months
Social behavior	Enjoys social give and take. Likes to play games such as being chased while creeping, hiding behind chairs, or waving "bye-bye." May be shy with strangers.	Likes to ride in his buggy and to go for short walks. Shows or offers toy.	Enjoys going for short walks. Dramatic imitative play—interested in household activities. Enjoys getting and putting things back for family members (21 months beginning of sense of property rights, "This is Daddy's; this is Bobby's").
Developmental Feeding	3 meals a day with midafternoon juice. Usually substitutes cup for bottle, or may combine the two. Can hold own cup. Can feed self with fingers. Often shows diminished appetite, especially when teething.	3 meals a day with midafternoon juice. Has discarded bottle. Attempts much self-feeding with fingers, spoon, and cup. Usually likes to feed self for one whole meal of the day.	Enjoys feeding himself and may be able to feed self. 3 meals with spilling, or may prefer to be fed by mother. Begins to show some preferences in foods and refuses others.
Sleep	Sleeps about 12 hours at night; usually 1 nap in middle of the day.	Sleeps about 12 hours at night; usually 1 nap in the early afternoon. (May wake at night and be frightened.)	Sleeps about 12 hours at night. 6–8 PM to 6–8 PM, nap in early afternoon of 1½–2 hours. Some night waking. (21 months—difficulties may be encountered in getting child to go to sleep, and disturbed sleep and night waking may be frequent.)

Dressing	Interested in helping take off hat, shoes, and pants. Cooperates in dressing—putting arms into armholes, extending legs to have pants put on, etc.	Not very interested in the dressing process as he is too interested in other things.	Interested and cooperative in dressing process. Can take off mittens, hat, socks, and unzip zippers. Tries to put shoes on. (21 months—is able to undress completely.)
Toilet training Bowel control		Some bowel control.	Some bowel control, often indicates toilet needs.
Bladder control	May remain dry during nap.	Partial toilet regulation. Responds to regular placements on toilet but does not indicate toilet needs and does not wait to be taken to toilet if need is not correctly anticipated. Toilet "accidents" are fairly common. Indicates wet pants.	Daytime regulation. Responds to regular toilet placements. The mother is able to keep the child dry all day with only rare "accidents." Does not indicate toilet needs but will wait some time for opportunity to use toilet.
Teeth	Usually 6 front teeth by the end of the first year (sometimes, however, as few as 2).		

Typical Behavior of Two-Year-Old Children

(Remember that every child develops according to his or her own rate of growth and in his or her individual way.)

	Two years	Thirty months
Motor behavior	Runs well, without falling, but still not very fast; leans slightly forward as he walks and runs. Walks up and down stairs alone, marking time; may use banister. Kicks and throws a ball. Chiefly interested in gross motor activity but has increased fine muscle control. Can now manipulate with one hand and alternates from one hand to the other. Can imitate a vertical and circular stroke. Likes to fit things together and take them apart. Better control of muscles of eyes and face than at 18 months.	Walks on tiptoe. Jumps with both feet in place. Tries to stand on one foot but loses balance. Holds crayon by fingers rather than in fist. Can imitate a horizontal stroke.
Language behavior	Uses personal pronouns, *I*, *me*, and *you*, but not necessarily correctly. Refers to self by name. Uses 2–3 word sentence or better. (Joins 2 words, noun, and verb at 18–21 months.) Number of words varies greatly, sometimes about 272. Asks for "another." Soliloquizes on his activities as he performs them. Verbalizes immediate experiences.	Repetitious speech—makes a remark over and over. Refers to self by pronoun rather than by name. May confuse *I* and *me*.

Mental behavior	Can identify parts of a doll—hair, ears, etc. Can fit forms into a formboard. Can obey 2 simple commands.	Can repeat 2 digits. Knows full name. Can fit forms into a formboard when rotated.
Social behavior	Beginning of parallel play—play alongside of other children, often engaging in the same activity but playing quite separately. Enjoys dollhouse play (domestic mimicry). Enjoys helping in the house—doing errands, setting table. Enjoys walks. Difficulty in understanding property rights—desires possessions of his own—"It's mine," constant refrain. Tends to hoard toys; difficulty in sharing. Calls all men and women Mommies and Daddies. May be shy with strangers, particularly adults. Father is often favorite, but also shows considerable dependence on mother.	Chiefly solitary and parallel play. Helps put toys away. Hard for children of this age to make choices. Difficulty in making transitions. Tends to be ritualistic—wants things always done in the same way. Likes short walks or rides in stroller. Enjoys short excursions to farms, likes to watch trains, etc. May go to extremes in behavior. Calls self *I* and has an increasing sense of *I*, especially in relation to immediate abilities. Calls other people *you*. Calls women *Lady* and men *Men*. Calls other children *Boys* and *Girls*. Knows he is a boy (or she is a girl). May show a preference for the father or mother. Usually can't enjoy 2 parents at once.

(continued)

Behavior of Two-Year-Old Children (continued)

	Two years	Thirty months
Developmental Feeding	Spoon grasped more between thumb and index finger and pronately, but there is still spilling. Is able to hold glass in one hand. Some children completely feed themselves, others want to be partially fed. Child usually has definite ideas of his likes and dislikes, may show "food jags."	Usually feeds self part of each meal. Likes repetition of foods and times at which certain foods are given. Has food preferences and may go on "food jags."
Sleep	6–8 PM to 6–8 AM. Usually a nap of 1–3 hours in afternoon; if not, child goes to sleep at about 6 or 7 PM. Much difficulty in going to sleep with many demands made for adult attention and occasional night-waking. Usually plays in bed for ½ hour before sleeping and upon waking in morning.	6–8 PM to 7–9 AM. Varies depending on length of nap. Nap varies from no sleep to 3, 4, 5 hours. Much of nap time may be spent playing in bed. May take ½ to 1 hour to get ready for bed (likes to follow a certain bedtime ritual). May awaken at night and usually has to be toileted at 10–12 PM.
Toilet training	Fewer daytime accidents. Dry at night if taken up. Verbalizes needs most of the time. Is able to differentiate bowel and bladder functions. (Girls usually achieve dryness sooner than boys.)	Rare daytime accidents. Most children need to be toileted during the night.
Dressing	Helpful and cooperative in dressing process. Pulls on simpler garments—mittens, pants—but has difficulty. Can undress completely. Enjoys washing and drying hands.	Attempts to dress self but gets socks and shoes on wrong, both feet in one pant leg, shirt backward, etc. Varies between desire to do complete dressing or to be completely dressed by parent.
Teeth	Usually 16.	Usually 20.

Typical Behavior of Three-Year-Old Children

(Remember that every child develops according to his or her own rate of growth and in his or her individual way.)

Motor behavior	Walks erectly with more balance than at 2 years, swinging arms in adult fashion. Walks up stairs, alternating feet. Rides tricycle. Can turn corners and stop abruptly. Stands on one foot, momentary balance. Increasing interest and ability in fine motor coordination—can draw a cross, copy a circle, fold paper crosswise or lengthwise.
Language behavior	Uses plurals, many verbs. Addition of 500–600 words per year, from 2–6 years, about 896 at 3 years. Knows a few rhymes. Likes to listen to words and acquire new words. Asks questions rhetorically: child knows the answer, but often asks a question because he or she wishes to be asked question. (Girls usually talk earlier than boys and are superior in language ability during the preschool years.)
Developmental Feeding	Feeds self well, with little or no spilling. Pours from pitcher. Less marked refusals and preferences for food than at 2 years. May like food which requires more chewing.
Sleep	May have difficulty going to sleep. May awaken often at night (sometimes needs to be fed and toileted). May be tired on awakening in morning. Usually takes a nap for 1–2 hours, but often may substitute a "play nap" for a real nap.
Toilet training	Assumes almost complete toilet responsibility, often sleeps dry through nap and night without being picked up or waked.
Dressing	Puts shoes on (not necessarily on correct feet), unbuttons front and side buttons, puts on socks, pants, sometimes sweaters and dresses. Cannot always tell front from back or fasten buttons.

(continued)

Typical Behavior of Three-Year-Old Children (continued)

Social behavior (continued)	child's favorite. Increasingly enjoys imaginative activity, often has an imaginary companion at 3½ years or plays at being an animal. Enjoys excursions and visits to other children's homes. Likes to watch men at work (carpenters, mechanics) and likes to watch steam shovels, cement mixers and other large machines. Good age for starting nursery school. Beginning of temporary attachments to one playmate, often of opposite sex (at 3–6 years).	Music	May reproduce whole songs, generally not in pitch. Begins to match simple tones. Can recognize several melodies. Likes to experiment with musical instruments. Marked individual differences in interest and ability to listen to music and in rhythmic ability—some children can gallop, walk, run, and jump in fairly good time to music. Enjoys a variety of musical experiences.
Toys	Toys for physical, imitative, manipulative, and creative play: Dolls, doll carriages, dishes, brooms; wooden animals; blocks; small cars; puzzles; pegboards with small pegs; paints, clay; crayons, carpentry; slides; swings; wagons; tricycles; dump trucks; climbing equipment; sand toys. Storybooks may be somewhat longer than at 2 years, with a picture on every other page.	Books	Increasing span of interest in listening to stories. Makes relevant comments about stories, relating them to own experience. Likes to look at books and "read" or explain the pictures. Enjoys stories about familiar experiences with repetition and imaginative stories based on real people and real animals such as *Caps for Sale*. Enjoys information books about nature or transportation in story form.

Mental behavior	Can repeat 3 digits. Limited sense of time. Can distinguish between night and day. Can understand "when it's time." Understands enough to wait a turn. Can tell the longer of two sticks or the bigger of two balls (at 3–6 years). Knows what to do when hungry or sleepy (at 3–6 years).
Social behavior	Solitary and parallel play with the beginning of spontaneous group play. Many pairings of children. Definite interest in other people. Capable of sympathy. Begins to understand taking turns and sharing toys. Less hoarding. Often can make simple choices between two alternatives. Tries to please and conform to cultural demands. Likes praise and friendly humor. More responsive to verbal suggestions from adults than at 2 years. Sense of *I* increasing. Combines self with another in use of *we*. Can tell difference between boys and girls, but makes no distinction in play. The mother is usually the

Creative ability Painting	Strokes are more varied and rhythmic than at 2 years; beginning of sense of design. May cover whole page with one color or with blocks of various colors. Works with more concentration and decision, and with joy and pride in product. May name finished product, but there is seldom any recognizable resemblance.
Finger painting	Experiments with whole hand and with finger movements. Some feeling for design.
Clay	Enjoys manipulating clay—patting, squeezing, making holes. Beginning of form—making flat cakes, balls, rolling long strips, etc. May name product.
Crayons	Enjoys variety of colors. May begin to make recognizable product earlier than in painting.
Blocks	Likes many shapes and sizes, order and balance in building. May combine with cars and other toys. Often names what is being made, but enjoys the process of construction more than playing with finished product.

Typical Behavior of Four-Year-Old Children

(Remember that every child develops according to his or her own rate of growth and in his or her individual way.)

Motor behavior	Can stand on one foot. Can hop on one foot. Can walk downstairs alternating forward foot. Can throw ball overhand. Can cut on a line with scissors.	Developmental Feeding	Begins to enjoy and to be able to eat with the family. Likes to help plan and prepare meals. Likes to set the table. May go on "food jags" or "food strikes," in the first part of year.
Language behavior	Knows about 1540 words. Use of complex and compound sentences becomes more common at 4½ years. Uses conjunctions, adverbs, expletives. Likes new, different words—silly words. Peak of questioning.	Sleep	Sleeps from 7 to 7. May have a "play nap" from 1 to 3 PM; seldom actually naps during day. Likes to spend 15–30 minutes in bed with a book or toys before going to sleep. Usually changes from crib to big bed.
Mental behavior	Can name objects from memory. Can discriminate forms and animals. Can count to two. Knows why we have houses and books. Can tell what a chair, dress, or shoe is made of (at 4–6 years). Can repeat 4 digits (at 4–6 years). Can tell likenesses and differences.	Toilet training	Most children able to assume complete responsibility. Some still need to be toileted during night.
		Dressing	Able to give himself most of bath. Able to dress and undress with little assistance. Knows front from back, can lace but not tie shoes, can button all but back buttons.

Social behavior	Creative ability	
Prefers to play more with other children rather than by self. More association group play than in early years, sometimes in groups of 3–4. Social dramatic play. Imaginative play more related to group than to solitary play (plays doctor or engineer more than animals). Likes to dress up and play being "grown up." Likes many varied activities. Particularly interested in excursions, short trips on train or bus, and picnics. Understands sharing toys—shares more with special friends than with other children. Proud of own possessions and products he makes. Age of barter and swapping possessions. Sometimes a tendency for play groups to divide into sexes—boys with boys, girls with girls; much playing together of both sexes, however. Expanding sense of self, indicated by bragging, boasting, and out-of-bounds	Painting	Holds brush in adult manner. Makes designs and crude letters—may draw horizontally. Draws objects with few details. Little size or space relationship—details most important to child drawn largest. Increase in verbal accompaniment explaining pictures. Beginning of self-criticism. Values product and wants to take paintings home.
	Finger painting	Experiments with fingers, hands, and arms in rhythmic manner. Some representation and naming.
	Clay	Uses large quantities; Increase in representation and imagination.
	Blocks	Cooperative in building in small groups. Makes complicated structures combining many shapes of blocks in symmetrical manner. Combines furniture and other equipment with structures for dramatic play. Likes to have finished project left standing.

(continued)

Typical Behavior of Four-Year-Old Children (continued)

Social behavior (continued)	behavior. Much more self-reliant but needs rules to which to conform. Especially enjoys doing things with the father. Strong feeling for family and home.
Music	Increase in voice control with more approximation to correct pitch and rhythm than at 3 years. May sing entire songs. Sings more in a group than formerly. Likes simple singing games and dramatizing songs. Increased spontaneity in rhythms. Likes to experiment with instruments. Creates songs during play.
Toys	Toys for imitative, creative, manipulative, and physical play: Housekeeping articles—dishes, cooking sets, ironing boards, and irons, tables and chairs, wash tubs, dolls; clay, paints, scissors, crayons, paste, carpentry (hammer, saw, nails, pieces of wood); blocks; puzzles; climbing equipment; swings; slides; tricycles; wagons; shovels; garden tools.
Books	Able to listen to stories in larger groups over longer period. High interest in words—silly words and play on words. Enjoys nonsense rhymes, rhyming poetry. Delights in humor and exaggeration in stories. Likes information books answering questions about his environment. Likes to make up and tell stories. Stories may be longer, include less pictures, and have more lines of text than at 3 years.

Typical Behavior of Five-Year-Old Children

(Remember that every child develops according to his or her own rate of growth and in his or her individual way.)

Motor behavior	Gross motor activity well developed. Can walk a straight line. Narrow stance, arms held near body. Walks downstairs alternating feet. Climbs with sureness. Adept at riding tricycle. Skips. Is able to throw and kick ball simultaneously. Increasingly more adept at fine muscle coordination—laces shoes, ties a knot or a bow, fastens buttons. Can copy a square, triangle, or figure eight. Usually definite handedness has developed—uses dominant hand and does not transfer objects from hand to hand.	Developmental Feeding	Eats part of meals with family group and feeds self. Enjoys simple foods (often dislikes cooked vegetables, puddings, casseroles). Beginning to use knife for spreading.
		Sleep	Sleeps from 7 to 9 PM to 7 to 8 AM (about 11 hours) and takes a ½ to 1 hour play nap with interesting play materials. May take 1 or 2 actual naps a week (boys usually nap more than girls). May dream and have nightmares with night waking. Usually can toilet himself at night.
		Toilet training	Assumes responsibility for toileting but may need an occasional reminder. Night accidents are rare, but night toileting is frequent.
Language behavior	Knows about 2,072 words. 4.6 words per sentence (from about 4½ years on).	Dressing	Is able to handle dressing and undressing, but may like assistance several days of the week. Can fasten all but back buttons. Many children are able to tie bows and shoe strings.
Mental behavior	Interested in copying letters and numbers. Can count to 4. Enjoys simple letter and number games. Learns during year to identify penny, nickel, dime. Attempts to add and subtract within 5. Beginning of sense of time—knows order		

(continued)

235

Typical Behavior of Five-Year-Old Children (continued)

Mental behavior (continued)	of events of day, days of week, may know order of days. May be interested in clock and like to get up by alarm clock. Knows age. Little insight into geographic relationships but recognizes specific landmarks. Can cross neighborhood streets and likes to do errands at the store. Memory for past events. Interested in reading-readiness activities during last part of year.	Creative ability Painting	Likes to paint, draw, color, paste, and especially cut. Plans picture before starting to paint. Needs and can handle more colors. Interested in the techniques of painting. Includes many minute details in pictures which are often recognizable. Likes to have pictures shown to the group to which he belongs, and may ask for a title or story to be written for it.
Social behavior	Prefers to play with children of own age. Tendency for some children to prefer to play with own sex, but will play with both sexes. Plays best with one child unless under supervision, but can play and work with a larger number of children than at 4. Can identify himself as part of a group and accept responsibility toward it. Can conform to a greater amount of group organization. Can abide by group rules. Likes to play best outdoors. More secure in sense of self than at 4—no longer brags—more calm, self-assured, and independent. Is tactful and anxious to	Crayons	Likes to make intricate designs which often have good balance and form. More complicated pictures with more details than his paintings. May tell a story about the picture.
		Clay	Enjoys manipulating clay but likes to plan a product, and includes many details such as adding a hat and other accessories to the body of a man.
		Blocks	Used for building roads, tracks, bridges, tunnels, fire engines, houses. May build with a group on a group project.

Category	Description	Category	Description
Social behavior (continued)	please. Imitates grownup behavior. Is able to take some responsibility. Shy in approach to people but is able to build up slow, steady relationships. Likes to prepare for future happenings. Here-and-now world most important, with interest in his own immediate experiences. Mother is usually the preferred parent, but is fond of father. Enjoys many types of games involving some group organization, particularly enjoys games requiring body activity.	Music	Enjoys listening to records and likes to play piano. Usually enjoys rhythmic activities, particularly dancing to music. Less creative in rhythmic activities than at 4—likes to follow an accepted pattern. Is able to identify various types of music and can change easily from one type of rhythm to another. Is able to sing a larger range of tones (about 10). Can identify high and low notes and tries to improve his tone. *However, there are wide individual differences in musical ability and rhythm.*
Books	Enjoys stories with repetitive action and phrases (animals, trains, fire engines). Interested in stories with more factual and scientific material than at 4. Stories may be personified (as long as animals act like animals, machines act like machines, etc., except for talking or thinking), because the 5-year-old can tell real from make-believe more easily than a 4-year-old. Stories may be quite long with many lines of text. 5-year-olds can listen almost twice as long as 4-year-olds, rarely interrupt, and don't need to participate in the story.	Toys	Toys for imitative, creative, manipulative, and physical play: Climbing equipment, tricycles, blocks, houses made out of blankets or tarpaulins, dolls and doll house equipment, dress-up clothes, sewing, carpentry (including simple tools), art materials, puzzles, simple beginning games such as lotto.

237

Characteristics of Children From 6 to 8 Years

Physical	Social	Emotional	Learning
1. Forty to 53 inches tall. (Average annual growth— 2 to 3 inches.)	1. Motor skill plays an important part in being accepted by child social groups.	1. Want love and affection from adults.	1. Have short attention span.
2. Weigh 36 to 66 pounds. (Annual average gain— 3 to 6 pounds.)	2. Are more interested in peer groups than in family group.	2. Take themselves seriously.	2. Like to experiment.
3. Rate of growth in height and weight slows down between ages 5 and 11, but there is a steady and uniform increase in size.	3. Form short-lived changing groups.	3. Are alternately aggressive and sympathetic.	3. Build experience into chains of ideas.
4. Legs lengthen rapidly.	4. Vacillate between working toward common end and intense personal rivalry.	4. Boys quarrel and use more physical force than girls.	4. Express simple reasoning with such phrases as "faster than" and "slower than."
5. Postural defects appear.	5. Are very social. Like to work and play with others but are beginning to be selective of friends.	5. Some children find satisfaction in fanciful companions.	5. Are not interested in attitudes or opinions, some thing "is" or "isn't."
6. Girls mature faster than boys.	6. Begin to show group loyalty—"us kids."	6. Show fear of imaginary creatures, witches, bogies.	6. Like rhymes, riddles, simple conundrums.
7. Exhibit extreme motor activity; emphasis in muscular activity is on speed and energy.	7. Seven- and 8-year-olds begin to have "girl and boy friends."	7. Show fear of being alone.	7. Are interested in free dramatic play.
8. Show gradual improvement in speed, steadiness of movement, and accuracy.	8. Boys have more lasting friendships.	8. Some show fear of criminal characters, funerals, characters from stories and pictures, remote animals, blood, death, fainting people.	8. Begin independent use of books and do more reading.
9. Are still physically dependent.	9. Styles of clothing, activities, language, and ideas are set by the group and	9. Girls show more fear than boys.	9. Enjoy reading stories about children like themselves.
10. Dentition is irregular; have baby, permanent,		10. Are actually frightened by certain events or by the association recalled by such events.	10. Prefer funny movies with children and animal characters.
			11. At six, tend to reverse letters such as *b* and *d*, to

and missing teeth.
11. Nose and throat difficulties are more frequent.
12. Resist taking a bath.
13. May take larger servings of food than stomach can hold.

are followed slavishly by its members.
10. Develop a recognition of the needs and the desires of other children.
11. Show independence by unacceptable language, dirty hands, tattered clothes.
12. Tell secrets, set up whispering and giggling campaigns.
13. Boast constantly.
14. Are highly competitive, independent, and self-assertive.
15. Generally have poor table manners.
16. Accuse adults of being too bossy, too strict, and not fair, and resist adult control.
17. Want group acceptance so much that they will ignore behavior codes set up by adults.

reverse meanings such as *come* and *go*, and to substitute words of the same general appearance.
12. Drawings are symbolic, gradually becoming realistic.
13. Show a marked interest in numbers.
14. Like nature and the fanciful.
15. Collecting interest is strong.
16. Like active, competitive games involving big-muscle activity, rough-and-tumble "horseplay."
17. Not particularly interested in team games.
18. Like to play house (both sexes).
19. Begin to like simple games, such as dominoes, "old maid."
20. Boys like blocks, wagons, running games; girls like dolls, playing school, ring games.

SOURCES OF INFORMATION ABOUT CHILD CARE
AND PROGRAMS FOR CHILDREN

Agency for Children, Youth & Families, U.S. Department of Health, Education and Welfare, Box 1182, Washington, D.C. 20013

American Academy of Pediatrics, P.O. Box 1034, Evanston, IL 60204

American Home Economics Association, 2010 Massachusetts Avenue NW, Washington, DC 20016

American Nurses Association, 2420 Pershing Road, Kansas City, MO 64108; 1030 15th Street NW, Washington, DC 20005

American Psychological Association, 1200 17th Street NW, Washington, DC 20036

Appalachian Regional Commission, 1666 Connecticut Avenue, NW, Washington, DC 20235

Association for Childhood Education International, 3615 Wisconsin Avenue NW, Washington, DC 20016

Bank Street College of Education, 69 Bank Street, New York, NY 10014

Black Child Development Institute, 1028 Connecticut Avenue NW, Washington, DC 20005

Child Development Associate Consortium, 805 15th St. NW, Suite 500, Washington, DC 20005

Child Study Association of America, 50 Madison Avenue, New York, NY 10028

Child Welfare League of America, 67 Irving Place, New York, NY 10003

Children's Defense Fund, 1763 R Street NW, Washington, DC 20009

Coalition for Children & Youth, 1910 K St. NW, Suite 800, Washington, DC 20006

Council on Social Work Education, 345 East 46th Street, New York, NY 10017

Day Care and Child Development, Council of America, 1012 14th Street NW, Washington, DC 20005

Educational Facilities Laboratory, 477 Madison Avenue, New York, NY 10022

Educational Resources Information Center (ERIC), Clearinghouse on Early Childhood Education, University of Illinois, 805 West Pennsylvania Avenue, Urbana, IL 61801

Government Printing Office, Washington, D.C. 20402. (Many documents published by various government agencies and departments can be obtained directly from the GPO.)

National Association for the Education of Young Children, 1834 Connecticut Avenue NW, Washington, DC 20009

National Association of Social Workers, 20 E Street NW, Washington, DC 20001

National Education Association, 1201 16th Street NW, Washington, DC 20036

National Federation of Settlements and Neighborhood Centers, 232 Madison Avenue, New York, NY 10016

National League for Nursing, 10 Columbus Circle, New York, NY 10019

United States Office of Education, Department of Health, Education and Welfare, Washington, DC 20201

Women's Bureau, United States Department of Labor, Washington, DC 20201

BIBLIOGRAPHY

Aaronson, M., & Rosenfeld, J. *Baby and other teachers.* Washington: Georgia Appalachian Outreach Project of the Day Care and Child Development Council of America, 1974.

Abstracts of state day care licensing requirements. Washington, D.C.: U.S. Department of Health, Education and Welfare, 1971. Volume I, *Family day care homes and group day care homes.* Volume II. *Day care centers* (DHEW, OCD Publications No. 72–12).

Addison, B. Evaluation of a training unit in the use of games and toys with day care mothers as part of a college course. Unpublished manuscript. Berkeley: Far West Laboratory, 1972.

Almy, M. *The early childhood educator at work.* New York: McGraw-Hill, 1975.

Ambron, S. R. *Child development.* San Francisco: Holt, Rinehart and Winston, 1975.

Auerbach, S. *Choosing child care: A guide for Parents.* San Francisco: Parents and Child Care Resources, 1976.

Auerbach, Stevanne. "What Mothers Want from Child Care." *Day Care & Early Education* Magazine Vol. 1 No. 4 New York April 1974.

Auerbach, Stevanne. "Day Care: The Forgotten Priority" *National Elementary Principal* Vol. 55 No. 6. July–August 1976.

Auerbach, Stevanne. "Child Care Services. Should the Public Provide Them? *Phi Delta Kappa.* Vol. 57 No. 8 Bloomington, Indiana, April 1976.

Bartholomew, R., McCord, S., Reynolds, H., & Stein, H. *Child care centers: Indoor lighting outdoor playspace.* New York: Child Welfare League of America, 1973.

Bell, T. H. *Your child's intellect: A guide to home-based pre-school education.* Salt Lake City: Olympus Publishing Company, 1972.

Berends, P. B. *Whole child whole parent.* New York: Harper's Magazine Press, in association with Harper & Row, 1975.

Blackwell, A. O., Cohen, C. W., Haynes, A. J., & Corbell, S. *Developing training support systems for home day care: Descriptive experiences with projections for future programs.* Denver: State of Colorado, Department of Education, 1973.

Bohmer, H. Why are we so reluctant about day care programs? A comparative appraisal. *Child Welfare,* May 1966, Vol. 45 No. 5 289–294.

Braga, L., & Braga, J. *Learning and growing: A guide to child development.* Englewood Cliffs, N.J.: Prentice-Hall, 1975.

Brazelton, T. B. *Toddlers and parents: A declaration of independence.* New York: Delacorte Press/Seymour Lawrence, 1974.

Brearley, M., & Hitchfield, E. A guide to reading piaget. New York: Schocken Books, 1970.

Broad, L. P., & Butterworth, N. T. The playgroup handbook: A world of activities for children 3 and up. New York: St. Martin's Press, 1974.

Building skills for day care of infants. New York: Institute for Child Mental Health, 1973.

Burnett, D. K. *Your pre-school child: Making the most of the years 2 to 7.* New York: Macfadden-Bartell Corporation, 1963.

Cauman, J. What is happening in day care: New concepts, current practices and trends. *Child Welfare,* 1956, *35,* 22–27.

Caldwell, B. M. The effects of infant care. *Review of child development research.* M. L. Hoffman & L. W. Hoffman (Eds.), New York: Russell Sage Foundation, 1964, pp. 9–88.

Caldwell, B. M. Can young children have a quality life in day care? *Young Children,* April 1973, *27,* Vol. 28 No. 4 197–208.

Caldwell, B. M., & Richmond, J. H. Appendix B: A "typical day" for the groups at the children's center. In L. L. Dittman (ed.), *Early child care: The new perspectives.* New York: Atherton, 1968, pp. 373–377.

Caldwell, B. M., Wright, C. M., Honig, A. S., & Tannenbaum, J. Infant day care and attachment. Presented at the 46th Annual Meeting of the American Orthopsychiatric Association, April 1969.

Child Care Bulletin No. 4: A survey of state day care licensing requirements. Social and Administrative Services Corporation. Washington, D.C.: Day Care and Child Development Council of America, 1971.

Child Care Bulletin No. 8: Zoning for day care (from models for day care licensing. Office of Child Development, Department of Health, Education and Welfare. Washington, D.C.: Day Care and Child Development Council of America, 1972.

Child Care Bulletin No. 9: Alternative federal day care strategies for the 1970's (Excerpts from the final report). Washington, D.C.: Day Care and Child Development Council of America, 1972.

Child care handbook. Washington, D.C.: The American Home Economics Association, 1975.

Child development in the home. Office of Human Development. U. S. Department of Health, Education and Welfare. Washington: U.S. Government Printing Office, 1974 (DHEW Publication No. (OOD) 74–42).

Class, N. E. *Licensing of child care facilities by state welfare departments: A conceptual statement.* Washington, D.C.: U.S. Department of Health, Education and Welfare, Children's Bureau, 1968 (Children's Bureau Publication No. 462).

Class, N. E. *Growing up in the 70's.* Sacramento: Assembly Office of Research, California Legislature, 1975.

Cohen, D. H., & Stein, V. *Observing and recording the behavior of young children.* New York: Teacher's College Press, 1969.

Collins, A. H. H. Some efforts to improve private family day care. *Children,* July 1966, Vol. 13 No. 4 135–140.

Collins, A. H. & Watson, E. L. The day care neighbor service: A handbook for the organization and operation of a new approach to family day care. Portland: Neighborhood Family Day System, 1969.

Collins, A. H. & Watson, E. L. Exploring the neighborhood family day care system. *Social Casework,* Nov. 1969, Vol. 50 No. 9 pp. 527–533.

Collins, A. H., & Watson, E. L. Summary of the day care neighbor service: Field study of the neighborhood family day care system. Unpublished manuscript. Portland: Neighborhood Family Day Care Program, 1969.

Compilation of state regulations for day care centers and group day care homes. Social and Administrative Services and Systems Association and the Consulting Services Corporation of Seattle. Seattle: National Day Care Licensing Study of the Office of Child Development, 1971.

Costin, L. B. New directions in the licensing of child care facilities. *Child Welfare,* Vol. 49 No. 2 pp. 64–71. Feb. 1970.

Crawford, C. H. A family day care program. *Child Welfare,* 1969, *48,* 160–162.

Dashe, M. (Ed.). *Children with special problems: A manual for day care centers.* Washington, D.C.: Day Care and Child Development Council of America, 1972.

Day care: An annotated bibliography. Urbana: Educational Resources Information Center, 1971.

Day care facts. Washington, D.C.: Women's Bureau, Employment Standards Administration, U.S. Department of Labor, 1973.

Day care licensing study: Summary report on phase I: State and local day care requirements. Washington, D.C.: U.S. Department of Health, Education and Welfare, 1973.

Designing the child development center. Project Head Start. Washington, D.C.: U.S. Department of Health, Education and Welfare, Office of Child Development, 1969 (OCD publication No. 0–369–699).

Dittman, L. L. (Ed.). *The infants we care for.* Washington, D.C.: National Association for the Education of Young Children, 1973.

Early childhood facilities/1: An annotated bibliography on early childhood. Ann Arbor: Architectural Research Laboratory of the University of Michigan, 1970.

Edwards, E. Family day care in a community action program. *Children,* 1968, *15,* 55–58.

Ellison, G. *Play structures: Questions to discuss/designs to consider/directions for construction.* Pasadena: Pacific Oaks College and Children's School, 1974.

Emlen, A. C. Boundaries of the surrogate relationship in family day care: An analysis of the caregiver role. Presented at the 51st Annual Meeting of the American Orthopsychiatric Association. San Francisco, April 1974.

Emlen, A. C., & Watson, E. L. *Matchmaking in neighborhood*

day care. Corvallis, Oregon: Continuing Education Publications, 1971.

Evans, E. B., & Sala, G. E. *Day care for infants: The case for infant day care and a practical guide.* Boston: Beacon Press, 1972.

Evans, E. B., Sala, G., & Evans, E. A. *Designing a day care center: How to select, design and develop a day care environment.* Boston: Beacon Press, 1974.

Evans, E. D. Contemporary influences in early childhood education. New York: Holt, Rinehart and Winston, 1971.

Feasibility report and design of an impact study of day care. Cambridge, Massachusetts: Center for the Study of Public Policy. Final report. Washington, D.C.: Office of Economic Opportunity, 1971.

Foley, F. A. Family day care for children. *Children,* 1966, *13,* 141–144.

Frost, J. L. *Revisiting early childhood education: Readings.* New York: Holt, Rinehart and Winston, 1973.

Goldsmith, C. A blueprint for a comprehensive community-wide day care program. Child Welfare, 1965, *44,* 501–503.

Griffin, A. *How to start and operate a day care home.* Chicago: Henry Regnery Company, 1973.

Grotberg, E. H. (Ed.). *Day care: Resources for decisions.* Washington, D.C.: Office of Economic Opportunity, U.S. Government Printing Office, 1971.

Guides for day care licensing. Washington, D.C.: Office of Child Development, U.S. Department of Health, Education and Welfare (DHEW Publication No. (OCD) 73–1053) 1971.

Hamilton, M. *Home based family services: Report of the Georgia outreach project.* Washington, D.C.: Day Care and Child Development Council, 1975.

Haggarty, R. J., Symposium: Does comprehensive care make a difference? *American Journal of Diseases of Children,* 1971, *122,* 467–482.

Haith, M. M. *Day care and intervention programs for infants.* Atlanta: Avatar Press, 1972.

Hendrick, J. *The whole child: New trends in early education.* Saint Louis: C. V. Mosby, 1975.

Honig, A. S., & Lally, R. J. *Infant caregiving: A design for training.* New York: Media Products, 1976.

How to operate your day care program. Wernersville, Pennsylvania: Ryan Jones Associates, 1970.

Huntington, D. S., Provence, S., & Parker, R. K. *Day care/2: Serving infants.* Washington, D.C.: U.S. Government Printing Office, 1971.

Infant care. U.S. Department of Health, Education and Welfare, Office of Child Development, Children's Bureau. Washington, D.C.: U.S. Government Printing Office, 1973.

Jameson, K., & Kidd, P. *Pre-school play.* New York: Van Nostrand Reinhold Company, 1974.

Keister, M. E. *The good life for infants and toddlers.* Washington, D.C.: National Association for the Education of Young Children, 1970.

Kritchevsky, S., Prescott, E., & Walling, L. *Planning environments for young children.* Washington, D.C.: National Association for the Education of Young Children, 1969.

Leeper, S., *Good schools for young children: A guide for working with 3, 4, and 5 year olds.* New York: Macmillan, 1968.

Levy, H. *The baby exercise book.* New York: Pantheon Books, 1973.

Lewis, M., & Rosenblum, L. A. (Eds.). *The effects of the infant on its caregiver.* New York: John Wiley and Sons, 1974.

Loda, F. A. Group care for children under 3: Experience with a program providing primary health care. Presented at the annual meeting of the American Public Health Association, October 28, 1970.

Loda, F. A., Glezen, W. P., & Clyde, W. A., Jr. Respiratory disease in group day care. *Pediatrics,* 1972, *49,* 428–437.

Manual on organization, financing and administration of day care centers in *New York City—for community groups, their lawyers and other advisers.* (2nd ed.). New York: Day Care Consultation Service of the Bank Street College of Education, 1971.

Markun, P. M. (Ed.). *Play: Children's business and a guide to play materials.* Washington, D.C.: Association for Childhood Education International, 1974.

Matterson, E. M. Play and playthings for the pre-school child. Baltimore: Penguin Books, 1973.

Milliken, M. E. *The care of infants and young children.* Raleigh, NC: North Carolina State Board of Education, 1967 (ERIC No. E91013 289).

Mindlin, R. L., & Densen, P. M. Medical care of urban infants: Health supervision. *American Journal of Public Health,* 1971, *61,* 687–697.

Murphy, L. B. Individualization of child care and its relation to environment. In L. L. Dittmann (Ed.), *Early child care: the new perspectives.* New York: Atherton, 1968, 68–104.

Nutrition and feeding of infants and children under three in group day care. Maternal and Child Health Service and Committee on Infant and Preschool Child, American Academy of Pediatrics. Rockville, MD: U.S. Government Printing Office, 1971.

Palmer, M. W. (Ed.). *Day care aides: A guide for in-service training.* New York: National Federation of Settlements and Neighborhood Centers, 1962.

Palmer, M. W. *Selected readings for day care aides: A guide for in-service training.* New York: National Federation of Settlements and Neighborhood Centers, 1962.

Parker, R. (Ed.). *The preschool in action: Exploring early childhood programs.* Boston: Allyn and Bacon, 1972.

Perlstein, M. H. *Flowers can even bloom in schools: Selected readings in educational psychology.* Sunnyvale, CA: Westinghouse Learning Press, 1974.

Provence, S. Guide for the care of infants in groups. New York: Child Welfare League of America, 1967.

Pringle, M. K. *The needs of children.* New York: Schocken Books, 1975.

Ruopp, R., O'Farrell, B., Warner, D., Rowe, M., & Freedman, R. *A day care guide for administrators, teachers, and parents.* Cambridge: MIT Press, 1973.

Sjolund, A. *Day care institutions and children's development.* Translated from Danish by W. G. Jones. Lexington: Saxon House/Lexington Books, 1973.

Suggestions for equipment for a day care classroom and ideas for equipping day care programs with materials available at minimal costs. Day Care Consultation Service. New York: Bank Street College of Education, 1971.

Tri-state guidebook for establishing child care centers. Tallahassee: Florida Department of Education, 1974.

Who cares for children? A survey of child care services in North Carolina. Durham, N.C.: The Learning Institute of North Carolina, 1974.

Willis, A., & Ricciuti, H. A good beginning for babies: Guidelines for group care. Washington, D.C.: National Association for the Education of Young Children, 1975.

Willner, M. *Magnitude and scope of family day care in New York City: Final Report.* Washington: U.S. Department of Health, Education and Welfare, Children's Bureau, 1966.

Willner, M. Unsupervised family day care in New York City. *Child Welfare,* 1969, *48,* 56–62.

INDEX